# THE LAST OF THE GREAT STATIONS

*40 Years of the Los Angeles Union Passenger Terminal*

Interurbans Special 72

**by Bill Bradley**

FRONT COVER PHOTOGRAPHS:

(Bottom left) Crowds converge on newly opened Los Angeles Union Passenger Terminal in May 1939. **Union Pacific**

(Top right) Santa Fe Railway steam locomotive No. 3782 awaits the green light in midafternoon, late 1940s. **Stan Kistler**

(Bottom right) The *Super Chief* is ready for departure from Los Angeles; City Hall's tower glows in the background. **Donald Duke**

BACK COVER PHOTOGRAPH:

Union Station's tile-roof buildings, with civic center behind, is seen from the track level. **Historical Collection, Security-Pacific National Bank**

# THE LAST OF THE GREAT STATIONS

© 1979 by Interurbans Publications

First Printing, Spring 1979

Library of Congress Catalog Number: 79-84387

ISBN: 0-916374-36-X

This book was manufactured in the United States of America. The text was set in 12 point Plantin Regular with captions set in 10 point Plantin Regular and headings in Palatino and Palatino Italic of various sizes. Printed on 100-pound Patina dullcoat.

Printed by G. R. Huttner Lithography
Burbank, California

*Union Pacific*

## Table of Contents

# INTRODUCTION

THE TITLE of this book explains just what Los Angeles Union Station is: the last in a series of grand, gilded train stations that were built in America before World War II during what might be termed the "Golden Age" of railroading. During this period when the railroads were at their peak as corporate giants, new terminals were conceived as status symbols far more than at any time before or since. Searching for an appropriate style, the architects found the lavish Beaux Arts or Neoclassical styles then in vogue to be most compatible with the railroads' aims. This extravagance reached its supreme manifestation in New York's fabled Pennsylvania Station, which was patterned after an ancient Roman Bath, and which occupied an entire city block, a station whose vast interiors would amaze us today had the structure not been torn down.

Union Stations, so named because they represented the "union" of more than one railroad in establishing a common facility, were generally the result of a different ego—this one civic instead of corporate—and were often included in schemes for civic improvement. In Washington, D.C., for example, Union Station was an integral part of the McMillan Plan of 1902 to upgrade the Mall and restore the capital to its original beauty. Similarly, in Los Angeles, civic leaders planned Union Station in conjunction with the Civic Center, hoping to eventually link the two with a wide, ceremonious Mall, and thus create a striking centerpiece for their fast-growing city.

The difference is that in Los Angeles, this dream for a union station became a noticeably significant issue. The city, after all, had acquired the status of a major city in a remarkably short period of time, and was therefore especially eager to possess the kind of railroad gateway that had become an established feature of older cities of similar size.

Although the structure that resulted was considerably less imposing than many of its predecessors, it nevertheless was conceived with an eye to opulence, and owed its more modest proportions to the style of architecture wished upon it by the city fathers who then, unlike today, regarded their city as primarily a center of tourism. For this reason, they wanted a station that would express the region's more marketable characteristics—including its Spanish heritage, its year-round climate and, above all, its mystique.

The irony is that by the time this long-standing dream became a reality, it was 1939, perilously close to when passenger trains would gradually slip away from their former glory. Not surprisingly, there were some individuals even then who were already speculating on the railroads' fate, and many went so far as to suggest that this train station might be the last of its kind to be built in America.

But however gloomy their predictions, the station opened its doors amid a fanfare befitting *Gone With the Wind*. And the promoters were undaunted in their proclamation that this opening would mark "a new epoch in the history of transportation in southern California." And so it opened on May 3, 1939. *Los Angeles Union Passenger Terminal*.

Too bad it was the last.

UNION STATION occupies a 45-acre site at 800 North Alameda Street, adjacent to the Los Angeles Civic Center. Looking northeast from City Hall, this 1953 view shows the site just after the Santa Ana Freeway was opened. *L.A.U.P.T.*

*Chapter 1*

# UNION STATION OPENS

FROM WEDNESDAY, May 3 to Friday, May 5, 1939, Los Angeles staged one of the biggest extravaganzas in its history to celebrate the opening of its new Union Station.

The festivities began with a parade down Alameda Street and continued with a formal dedication, tours of the station, some side entertainment and a show entitled, "Romance of the Rails," which was presented several times daily in a specially constructed amphitheatre on the station's tracks.

More than half a million people showed up for the parade, and many of them were so unchecked in their enthusiasm that it took police 40 minutes to clear them from the street so the parade could proceed.

Los Angeles had campaigned long and hard for this station, and it was determined that its opening would not go by without a proud roar.

THESE TRAINS representing the Santa Fe, Southern Pacific and Union Pacific railroads figured prominently in the festivities which opened Union Station. All decked out in flags, they posed on the station's tracks for public viewing after rolling down Alameda Street in the parade. *Melching Brothers*

THE PARADE began at 11:40 a.m., May 3, and proceeded along Alameda Street from Eighth Street to the front of the station, where it passed a reviewing stand made up of civic leaders and officials representing the railroads. Leading the parade were the massed colors of the American Legion, followed by army trucks from the 63rd Coast Artillery. Then came floats from major companies—including the *Los Angeles Times*—and surrounding communities, all keyed to the theme, "Railroads Build the Nation." For music, there were some 10 marching bands—including the Southern Pacific band from San Francisco and the then-renowned Santa Fe All-Indian band from Winslow, Arizona. The bulk of the parade, however, focused on the history of transportation, and climaxed with appearance of rolling stock from the three railroads serving the city, symbolizing their joint effort in the Union Station undertaking.

AT THE CONCLUSION was this formal dedication ceremony. Speaking at the reviewing stand (at far left of picture on facing page) were presidents of the three railroads, Los Angeles Mayor Fletcher Bowron and California Governor Culbert Olsen (left). ***Both: Union Pacific***

(Above) SCREEN STAR Leo Carillo was a featured guest during Old-Timers' Night on the evening of May 2, 1939, when a banquet was held at the station honoring veteran employes of the railroads. Everyone present was dressed in costumes representing the early days of Los Angeles. ***Union Pacific***

"... Dedicated to the spirit of private enterprise and the continuing growth of Southern California"

THE NATIVE Daughters of the Golden West staged this reception in the terminal on May 3. Featuring refreshments and entertainment, it was but one small part of the three-day celebration.
***Both: Union Pacific***

# UNION STATION
# CELEBRATION COMMITTEE

WALDO T. TUPPER, *Managing Director*

PRESENTS

# "ROMANCE OF THE RAILS"

## California's Story of Transportation

*Written and Directed by* JOHN ROSS REED

## GRAND FINALE

*"Railroads Build the Nation"*

Wesley Givens, *Stage Director*
Henry Caubison, *Associate Director*
Steve Clark, *Production Manager*

Adolph Tewes, *Stage Manager*
Herb Wilkins, *Musical Director*

Jack Boyle, *Equestrian Director*
Piano—So. Calif. Music Co.
Otto K. Olesen, *Lights*

Narrators . . . The Man—Raine Bennett       The Woman—Jane Goude

Research . . . Earl I. Hall - Raine Bennett

### ACKNOWLEDGMENTS

The Executive Committee and Staff of "Romance of the Rails" thankfully acknowledge the generous cooperation of the following individuals and organizations:

Atchison, Topeka and Santa Fe Railroad
Southern Pacific Company
Union Pacific Railway
Pacific Electric Railroad
Los Angeles Railway

Cecil B. DeMille Productions
Paramount Pictures, Inc.
Universal Pictures Company, Inc.
Federal Theatre Project

Twentieth Century-Fox Film Corporation
Raoul de Ramirez
The Meglin Studios
Boy Scouts of America
Railroad Boosters Club

*Our sincere apology to any deserving name which might have unintentionally been omitted from the above list.*

*Gerald M. Best*

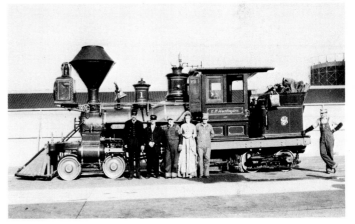

THE SHOW, "Romance of the Rails," was staged in front of a 6,000-seat amphitheatre and featured narration, music from a men's chorus of railroad workers and elaborate staging to depict the history of Southern California and its development through transportation. A few scenes are shown on the next three pages, with captions from the show's program. *Ralph Melching*

*"The last rail needed to complete the greatest railroad enterprise in the world is about to be laid; and the last spike needed to unite the Atlantic and the Pacific is about to be driven."*

*Union Pacific*

Promontory Point, Utah—1869

The Southern Pacific—September 6, 1876

This locomotive is the Southern Pacific's veteran
*C.P. Huntington.* ***Melching Brothers***

The Horse Car

This is being drawn by a Southern Pacific shop
switcher. ***Melching Brothers***

Grand Finale—"Railroads Build the Nation"

These steam trains lumbered in for the finale, and were routinely greeted by a standing ovation. *Melching Brothers*

## Rail Goliaths

The three railroads each provided one of their large locomotives for the parade and "Romance of the Rails" show.

(Top) By the time Santa Fe's No. 5006 approached the depot with its train of display cars, it had taken on hundreds of "guests." The police could not cope with them, so many took this once-in-a-lifetime ride in the terminal. *Gerald M. Best*

(Middle) Union Pacific sent its *Challenger* type No. 3939, bedecked in California state banners. *Melching Brothers*

(Bottom) A Southern Pacific streamlined *General Service* steamer arrived in a sea of American flags. *Melching Brothers*

LOTS OF CREATIVE "MAKE-BELIEVE" went into creating vintage trains for the "Romance of the Rails" show. Lacking real stock, the railroads turned to Hollywood's motion picture techniques.

(Top right) The Union Pacific train actually consisted of Virginia & Truckee locomotive No. 22, posing as "Union Pacific 22," pulling ex-Virginia & Truckee coach No. 4.

(Middle) Southern Pacific's "old-time entry" was its own historical locomotive, the *C.P. Huntington*, with ex-Virginia & Truckee coach No. 3 lettered as "Southern Pacific Lines 1."

(Bottom right) Shopmen at the Santa Fe Railway took saddle-tank steamer 2267 and mounted old-fashioned fixtures such as a diamond smokestack, headlight and wooden pilot to create "AT&SF 567," which towed another ex-Virginia & Truckee coach (lettered "Santa Fe 24") in the pageant. ***ALL: Gerald M. Best***

MILITARY MIGHT was one of the features of the opening celebration parade down Alameda Street. A special train, pulled by a shiny Southern Pacific cab-forward locomotive, carried many helmeted U.S. Army troops on flat cars and military box cars. Centerpiece of the train was this huge railway gun from Ft. MacArthur. ***Gerald M. Best***

## Preview of Coming Attractions

The movie people had the honor of running the first train out of Union Station. It was a publicity stunt not witnessed by the public. On April 24, 1939, Paramount gathered a group of stars and starlets at the brand new terminal to send off a special train that would operate a 10,000-mile circuit across the nation to promote *Union Pacific,* its latest cinematic epic. In the view at left, the three gentlemen in the foreground are (l. to r.) Los Angeles Mayor Fletcher Bowron, Union Pacific Railroad President Jeffers, and famed Paramount director Cecil B. DeMille. Among the many Hollywood luminaries we recognize (top row) George Raft, Lynne Overman and, at far right, Lloyd Nolan. ***Gerald M. Best***

Two types of motive power pulled the movie special. At left is ex-Virginia & Truckee No. 18 (now lettered as "Union Pacific 58"), built in the Central Pacific railroad shops in 1873. It received new engine and tender truck wheels and bearings as well as new rod and driver axle bearings for the 10,000-mile trek. Behind the ancient steamer, two brand-new General Electric turbo-electric locomotives combined to give enough power for the tonnage. No. 1, seen at right, had been delivered just a month before. ***BOTH: Gerald M. Best***

*Chapter 2*

# TWENTY YEARS OF TUMULT

IT WAS AN ORDINARY train, certainly not the flagship of any railroad's fleet. But it achieved a place in transportation history when, with the earliest rays of the rising sun on the morning of May 7, 1939, Southern Pacific's *Imperial* became the first revenue passenger train to arrive at Los Angeles Union Station. The *Imperial* did not have glamor; its utilitarian appearance did not match the grace and beauty of the great Spanish-Mediterranean terminal. Its passengers came from such places as El Centro, Calexico, Yuma and points east.

But it was a moment to remember, and of the *Imperial's* 100 passengers, 20 or so—mostly railfans—jumped onto the platform that 5:30 a.m. in a mad scramble to be "first" to set foot into the new station. Behind now were 20 years of struggle to build the station, to create a fitting front door for the City of the Angels. Ahead were 20 years of tumult,

Donald Duke

FIRST DAY'S OPER-ATION, Sunday, May 7, 1939, witnessed Santa Fe (left) and Southern Pacific (right) steam locomotives and long trains, both traditional heavyweight and new-fangled streamliners.
*Melching Brothers*

of crowds, of war and its terrific impact on passenger travel, of glory for the great trains such as the *Lark,* the *Super Chief,* the *City of Los Angeles.*

It all started modestly enough. For the first three years of its operation, Union Station served some 7,000 passengers daily and maintained a staff of 325, not counting employees of the railroads themselves who sold the tickets, or of Railway Express and the Pullman Company, who were tenants. The first terminal timetable, effective May 7, 1939, listed 33 arrivals and 33 departures. This was to be the norm for some 20 years, not counting the peak of World War II when LAUPT employee ranks swelled to some 1,000 and as many as 100 trains a day struggled to carry an unprecedented passenger load. Trains were "SRO" during the war—standing room only. It became necessary to add facilities for members of the armed services, and there were times when men in uniform seemingly outnumbered the civilians at the station.

Business returned to normal after the war—actually better than normal for some time, since the station had opened

(Facing page) HEAVY CROWD of passengers—mostly servicemen—struggles toward a rendezvous with Union Pacific's *Challenger* to Chicago, June 15, 1943. World War II days taxed the terminal to its utmost. **Union Pacific**

when the nation was still recovering from a recession which cut into passenger travel. In 1948, the station was still handling 66 revenue trains per day, plus extra sections (see following section). But events were taking place here and elsewhere which were to damage, and eventually all but destroy, the importance of LAUPT as the city's gateway to the traveling public.

As soon after World War II as possible, the city of Los Angeles spent large sums of public money to improve Mines Field in Inglewood and turn it into what eventually became Los Angeles International Airport. Airlines moved their operations there from such suburban locations as Glendale and El Monte, and Douglas introduced the DC-6 airliner. The skyway was coming of age, and since time is always money, the businessman soon had no more time for the train. Union Station's slow toboggan ride to oblivion began on September 27, 1953, when two of the 66 daily trains came off the timecard. Two more were discontinued on June 6, 1954. Effective January 9, 1955, only 58 trains (29 in, 29 out) were being operated. On April 24, 1955, it was down to 56. None of the premier trains was discontinued, but some of the secondary runs were dropped or combined. Early victims were the Santa Fe's "motor" locals to San Bernardino via both Pasadena and Fullerton.

Further abscission of the station's train services occurred in 1956 and 1957, and by September 28, 1958, the time-card had shrunk to only 46 daily trains (23 in and 23 out). By 1961 four more trains had vanished. It was now obvious that fundamental changes in America's travel habits were taking place, and that Union Station would suffer more—much more.

The final blow came late in 1959 with the introduction of the Boeing 707 into regular service. Union Station, long the main point of entry and departure for the long-distance traveler, finally lost out completely to the emerging jetport west of Inglewood. And without any rail commuter traffic, a feature which kept older terminals in the east alive, the station all but closed its doors on a passing era.

By 1967, there were only 15 arrivals and 15 departures daily from Union Station—less than half the number on opening day. Two years later, the daily train activity was down to just 18 trains a day, nine in, nine out. Six of these 18 were *San Diegans* which the Santa Fe had nearly given up on, even though that would later prove to be premature. The patrician *Super Chief* still ran, but suffered the indignity of hauling the *El Capitan's* coaches behind its first-class cars. The lordly overnight *Lark* was gone and the *Coast Daylight* was a ghost of its former greatness.

In the station itself, the Harvey House closed, as did the cocktail lounge, the barber shop and other pasenger amenities. Not even veteran railroad employees knew what to expect now. One thing they knew for sure was that Union Station had fallen on hard times. The question now was whether anyone really cared.

(Left) JUST A FEW FEET AWAY from the milling masses was this patio hideaway, where passengers could relax while awaiting departure time. **Southern Pacific**

(Right) RECRUITS FROM Great Lakes Naval Training Station head into the terminal, August 3, 1940. **Union Pacific**

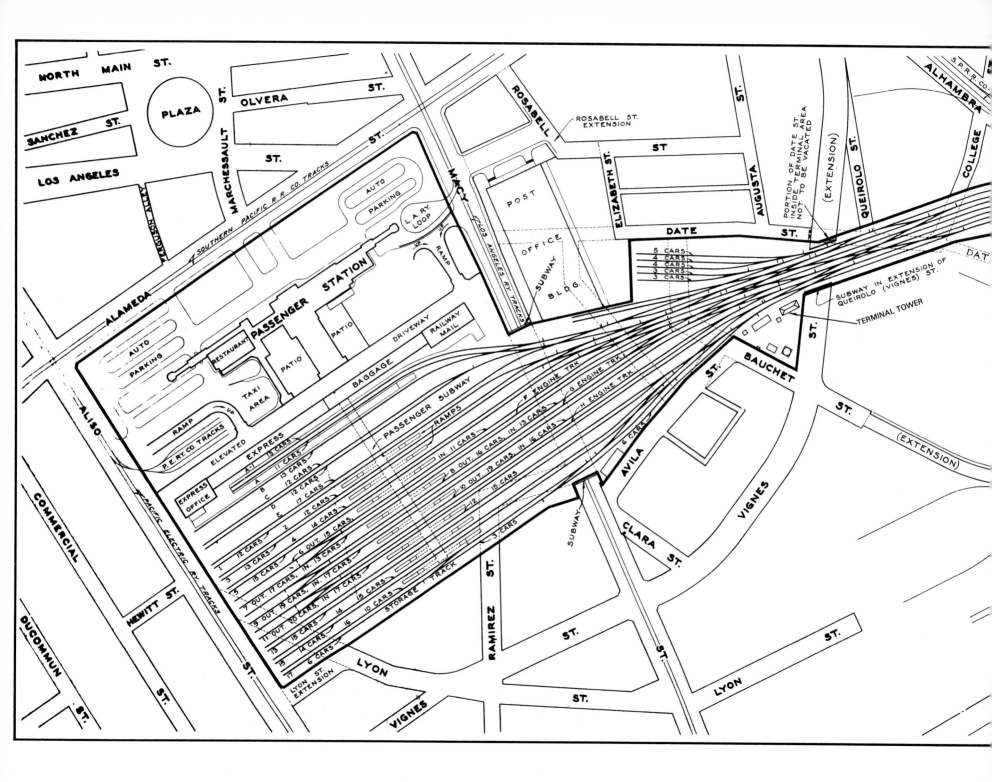

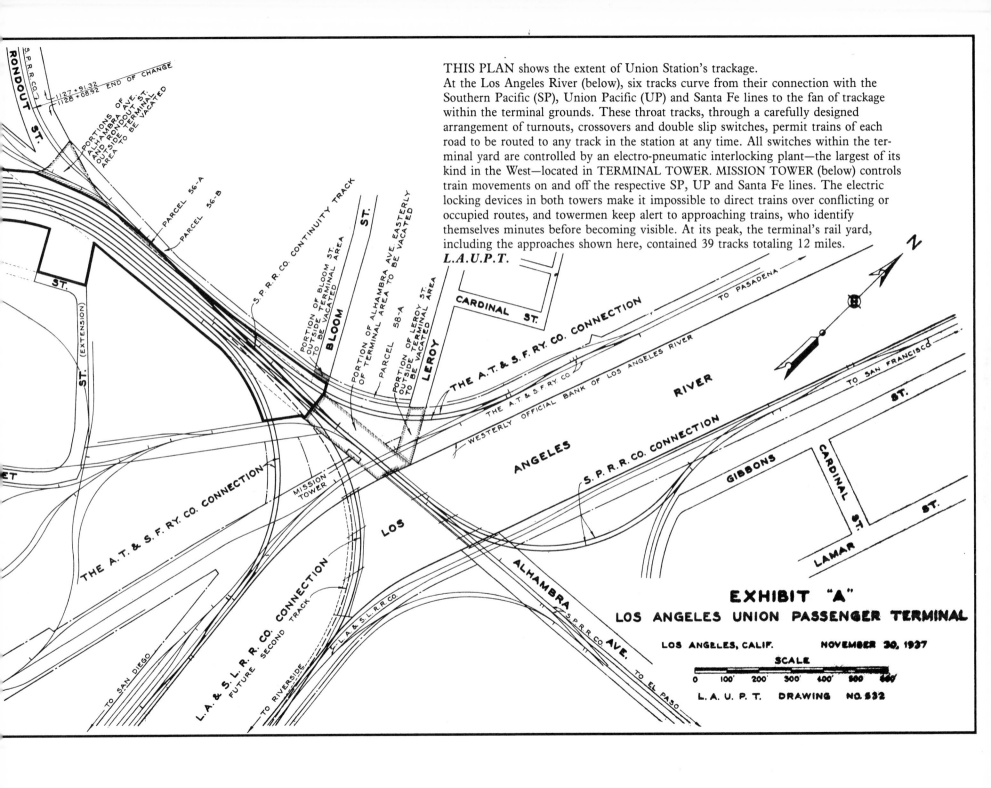

THIS PLAN shows the extent of Union Station's trackage.
At the Los Angeles River (below), six tracks curve from their connection with the Southern Pacific (SP), Union Pacific (UP) and Santa Fe lines to the fan of trackage within the terminal grounds. These throat tracks, through a carefully designed arrangement of turnouts, crossovers and double slip switches, permit trains of each road to be routed to any track in the station at any time. All switches within the terminal yard are controlled by an electro-pneumatic interlocking plant—the largest of its kind in the West—located in TERMINAL TOWER. MISSION TOWER (below) controls train movements on and off the respective SP, UP and Santa Fe lines. The electric locking devices in both towers make it impossible to direct trains over conflicting or occupied routes, and towermen keep alert to approaching trains, who identify themselves minutes before becoming visible. At its peak, the terminal's rail yard, including the approaches shown here, contained 39 tracks totaling 12 miles.
*L.A.U.P.T.*

EXHIBIT "A"
LOS ANGELES UNION PASSENGER TERMINAL
LOS ANGELES, CALIF.    NOVEMBER 30, 1937
SCALE
0   100'   200'   300'   400'   500'   600'
L.A.U.P.T.   DRAWING   NO. 532

AT MISSION TOWER, 94 working levers control the following: 12 derails, 28 turnout switches, six double slip switches, two turnout switches with movable point frogs, and 16 crossovers. Ninety-six more levers control 96 signals, and five levers control nine electric locks on switches that are not used frequently enough to warrant the expense of interlocking and handling from the tower. Seen here in 1947 is Santa Fe Towerman, E.L. Kelly, whose job also includes coordinating movements with the station's Terminal Tower. *Stan Kistler*

IN THE TERMINAL'S rail yard, eight passenger platforms (marked by the "butterfly" sheds ahead) are set among 16 tracks. Six additional tracks, located nearest the station, are reserved for express and baggage loading. The Post Office Terminal Annex is off the picture to the right. *Stan Kistler*

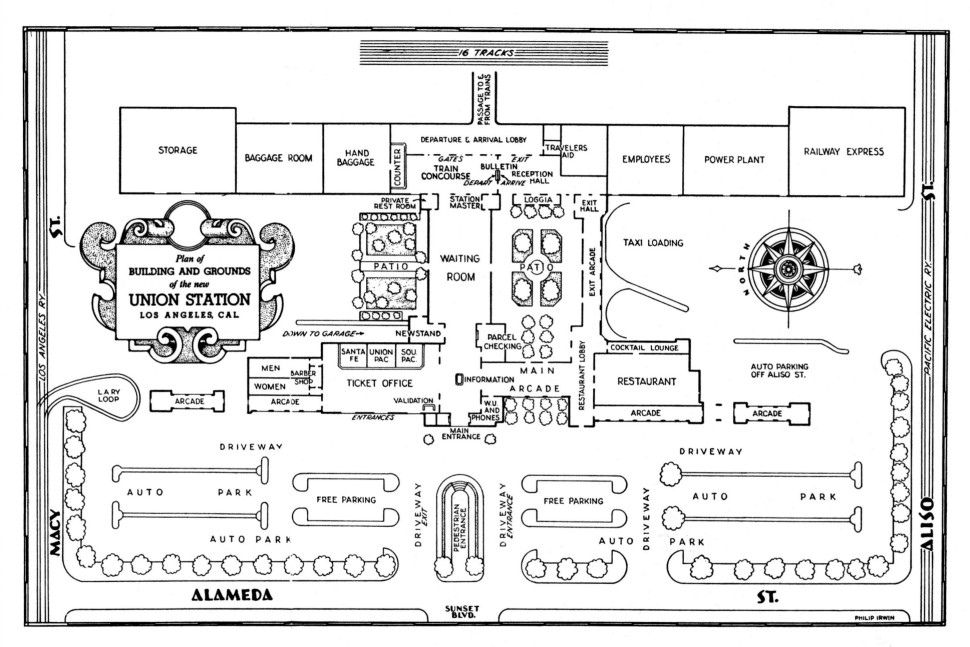

AS THIS FLOOR PLAN indicates, everything in the station is laid out for maximum efficiency. Passengers are separated from the tracks by an underground corridor. This is linked to the platforms by eight sets of double ramps. The main building occupies an area of 78,019 square feet; the baggage and express units occupy 199,549 square feet. Parking is available for 478 cars on surface lots, while an underground garage provides space for 123 more.

IN THE DAYS before Amtrak, Union Station was run by a three-man board of managers comprising the western managers of the owning railroads. Operating costs were allocated among the three railroads on a car-use basis, taking into account the number of cars and locomotives run into and out of the station by each road. Depending upon the year, Santa Fe and Southern Pacific were the biggest users, with Union Pacific a distant third. Los Angeles County *ad valorem* taxes for the station were $3.5 million in 1939; $7,996,994.69 in 1958-59. ***Union Pacific***

PLATFORM SCENE was taken on June 23, 1949, and shows members of the Railway Club of Southern California boarding a "Summer Holiday" excursion.
*Stan Kistler*

## Noontide of a Great Station

TODAY'S JET SET considers the airport to be the focal point for the comings and goings of our mobile society —the city gate for the millions who start and end their journeys on the public conveyances of a generation in a hurry. And rightly so, especially on the West Coast where the intercity passenger train no longer plays much of a role in overland travel.

In Los Angeles, it's LAX. The very initials, once meaningful only to baggage clerks and airline pilots, have entered the common vocabulary: LAX—Los Angeles International Airport. It's where everybody goes, if they're going somewhere.

It used to be LAUPT.

Not that the initials LAUPT ever meant much to the traveling public, especially in a more leisurely era when people were less inclined to take shortcuts, even in conver-
sation. But LAUPT meant "Los Angeles Union Station" (actually, Los Angeles Union Passenger Terminal, as its railroad owners referred to it), and that's where the action was.

Today's airport traffic jams, ticket counter lines, baggage waits, quick cups of coffee and gulped sandwiches used to be downtown, at the station. LAX was just a pasture—Mines Field—home to a few private planes and an occasional barnstorming dirigible. It wasn't until after World War II that LAX became an important point of intercity embarcation, and for a few years LAX and LAUPT co-existed, each handling sizable crowds. But the pendulum was swinging. Swinging away from the train sheds, the tracks, locomotives and the steel wheel on the steel rail. The swing was barely noticeable at first.

Let's go back in time to when LAUPT was still young, still vibrant, still important. Still a beehive of activity. A time not so long ago when the traveling salesman, overnight bag in hand, was likely to tell the cab driver "Union Station" without so much as a second thought.

Let's pick a day—say February 29, 1948. Leap Year Day. A day in the life of Los Angeles Union Station. More than 1,000 employees kept the huge station pulsing with life every minute of the 24-hour day the year that Harry Truman defeated Thomas E. Dewey to keep his job as President of the United States. Harry Truman liked trains. Rode them a lot. Campaigned on them, and in crisscrossing the country pulled a political upset. His campaign train visited LAUPT, too. Many important trains did. It was not only a very busy transportation temple, it was important and prestigious. Important enough, in fact, to prompt the biggest stars in the Hollywood movie firmament to sneak off the Super Chief at the suburban Pasadena stop, to avoid being mobbed by the crowds at LAUPT.

Even the unimportant were mobbed by the crowds at LAUPT, because it was a mighty busy place. On Leap Year Day, 1948, sixty-six trains entered and left the station every 24 hours; 33 departures and 33 arrivals. If that doesn't sound impressive, consider for a moment that most of the trains were long, heavy transcontinental or transcoastal "name trains" each carrying 10 to 20 coaches and Pullmans. Some simple arithmetic suggests that even if the average train carried only 200 passengers, some 13,200 people per day used LAUPT as their portal for the city. And on many days, the total was easily two or three times that number. In the context of the size of the city then, and the reduced economic circumstances, these were very impressive figures even in the light of today's LAX mob scenes.

One factor that LAUPT lacked, that most of the other great American railroad terminals had, was commuter traffic. Except for a handful of locals, all travel in or out of LAUPT consisted of through passengers, and no railroad has in modern times offered regular commuter service from Los Angeles in the traditional sense: cheap, multi-ride tickets, peak-hour scheduling, suburban stations, etc. Had even a modest commuter schedule been superimposed on LAUPT's through scheduling, its eight platforms would have carried an even more impressive crush of humanity.

The great trains were, of course, just a part (one might even say a small part) of the activity of Union Station. The logistical support needed to operate LAUPT was considerable: locomotive sheds, off-premises railway car storage, switchmen, towermen, signal maintainers, dispatchers, policemen, porters, ticket sellers, information clerks, cooks, ushers, gatemen, janitors, freight and express handlers, employes of such allied services as the Pullman Company, Railway Express Agency, and even the U.S. Post Office Department whose giant Terminal Annex across the street was actually an integral part of the station's activities.

A great gateway never closes its doors.

TODAY, LEAP YEAR DAY, 1948, begins at midnight. The great halls of the station, the ticket lobby and waiting room, are comparatively peaceful now, the constant sound of voices down to a murmur. A few Yellow Cabs wait by the South Portico, but business is slack and the drivers lounge in small groups or grab a quick coffee at the Fred Harvey lunch counter.

Behind the scenes, things are busier. Away from the terminal, crews of the Southern Pacific, Santa Fe and Union Pacific yards are servicing the coaches that will make up the early morning trains, while Pullman crews stock their cars with fresh linens and the commissary is busy with long lists of provisions to be provided the diners and lounges in the consists of the day's trains. At the roundhouses, a few miles away, giant steam and diesel locomotives are being groomed for their forthcoming runs.

It's a chilly night; February in Los Angeles can be downright cold, swaying palm trees notwithstanding. LAUPT's

boiler room is going full blast, providing steam heat for the giant terminal and its drafty expanses. The city is quiet now. Late moviegoers are still on their way home, but in all departments at LAUPT supervisors are busy making up the day's duty rosters, planning the administration of the new day when 33 trains will come and 33 trains will go, and the rails will never be still.

Next door, the Terminal Annex, its interior lights ablaze, is the scene of intense activity. Mail is being readied for the early morning dispatches, with most trains carrying either Railway Post Office cars where the mail will be sorted en route, or at least closed pouch cars for bulk mail movement to outlying points. Midnight has brought scarcely a lull, after the 11:30 p.m. departure of Santa Fe's Number 8, the long and heavy transcontinental mail train which left from a track nearest the Annex with mail and express for Chicago and points east. Number 8 carries three full Railway Post Office cars, a number of closed pouch cars and enough

express to make up, frequently, a full 16-car train of heavy-weight equipment. On the end of Number 8 is a "rider coach," a combine coach with seats for perhaps 20 passengers at the most. Of course, since the Santa Fe doesn't advertise Number 8 in its timetables, few passengers are carried; none is wanted. Number 8 is the Santa Fe's fastest train—faster than the Super Chief. But that speed is reserved for first-class mail and packages.

While the post office hums, so does the Railway Express Agency. All the previous day, REA's green trucks have been shuttling across the Southland, picking up packages for distant points. At the south end of LAUPT, parcels have been collected and sorted and made ready for dispatch on many of the trains which will depart LAUPT early in the day. Even the crack trains carry baggage and express cars, and some of the trains carry many—more packages than people. In 1948, the "head end" business is, in fact, what keeps many of the trains alive, since the automobile has long since cut deeply into the day coach trade.

Out at the very south end of the LAUPT grounds, there is a very noisy—and interesting—freight operation going on. A railroad within a railroad. The Pacific Electric—Los Angeles' "Big Red Car" system—maintains a four-track yard leading from its Aliso Street passenger tracks. The curves are sharp—and throughout the evening those curves have felt the squealing flanges of the PE's large "box motor" fleet, bringing more packages into LAUPT for trans-shipment onto the mainline trains.

LAUPT is, in fact, one of Pacific Electric's three main Box Motor terminals. The other two are at the Eighth Street Yard and the Baggage and Mail Room beneath the elevated at PE's Sixth and Main Station. So important is LAUPT to PE's package express network that all box motor activity is governed by an Assistant Trainmaster at LAUPT. These red box motors, looking very much like their Big Red Car cousins except for a lack of windows on

the side, have been trundling in from such outlying points as San Bernardino, Santa Ana, Long Beach and even Santa Monica, slowly making their way up the busy San Pedro Street trackage to bring their cargos to Union Station. In many parts of the nation, such local rail-borne express service is a thing of the past, but not in Los Angeles where the PE network is still largely intact and functioning in a big way. Some say it won't last, but today, Leap Year Day, it is important. At the small but incredibly busy LAUPT box motor yard, loading and unloading is performed by Railway Express crews.

Throughout the night, the work continues, mostly behind the scenes. About 3 a.m., a terminal cop gently escorts an unsteady customer off the premises; the station cocktail bar had closed on schedule, but apparently this gentleman had continued to imbibe from a handy coat-pocket source until his staggering caught the attention of a porter. But the station's handsome carved wood and leather seats continued to

TWO ELECTRIC RAIL-WAY systems served Union Station, one at either end. (Above) Looking at the north end of the station were cars of the Los Angeles Railway (later Los Angeles Transit Lines), which deposited passengers just a few steps fron the ticket counter. (Right) The Pacific Electric box motor yard was at the south side of the station near the power plant. Express and parcels from outlying points rode the Red Car system direct to Union Station for shipment onto mainline trains. This operation ended in 1951.

JUST BEHIND THE locomotive is the Utility Building, a two-and three-story structure which extends along the entire length of the platforms, acting as a bridge between them and the terminal building. In the '40s and '50s, this building handled all baggage, mail and express. Baggage carts moved up to train level from the street on a curving ramp (off the picture at right). *Donald Duke*

comfort a scattering of snoozing passengers, left undisturbed for the night. A few had arrived on the 12:30 a.m. Santa Fe San Diego local, and would depart on early morning trains. A night in a hotel was an unnecessary extravagance, so LAUPT obliged with an upholstered chair.

And so the night wears on. Then, before the first rays of the morning sun begin to filter in through the tall concourse windows, the tempo picks up. The first early morning streetcars squeal around the narrow-gauge Los Angeles Transit Line loop at the north end of the ticket hall; most of the disembarking riders are terminal employees, but some have come to catch early trains. Likewise, the taxi ranks thicken out front, and suddenly the station's corps of Red Caps has assembled. The station's tile floors now ring to the footfalls of people in a hurry. The real day has begun.

The pedestrian tunnel under the platforms, up to now nearly deserted except for the occasional train crewman or

night watchman, swells with activity at the simultaneous 6 a.m. arrival of Southern Pacific train 56, the *Tehachapi*, and departure of SP 71, a maid-of-all-work San Francisco local. Number 56 has made its way from Oakland down the San Joaquin Valley route, and made its way slowly indeed, having left Oakland 20 hours before. Very much a secondary train, number 56 was meant for parcels instead of people. SP number 71 is very much the same, except that it will take the more scenic Coast route. And it will make a lot of stops.

Out on the platforms, the short lull between 6 and 7 a.m. is contrasted with the continued quickening of activity within the station itself. The Harvey restaurant is jammed, and not only with train passengers and LAUPT employees, but with customers on their way to places of work nearby. The Fred Harvey company serves very good food, indeed, and the Harvey Girls are dispensing their customary alert brand of service. The crowd soon spreads across the main

# LOS ANGELES UNION PASSENGER TERMINAL
# TIME TABLE

**Effective February 29, 1948**

| | ARRIVING | | | LEAVING | |
|---|---|---|---|---|---|
| **TRAIN** | **TIME** | **NAME** | **TRAIN** | **TIME** | **NAME** |
| SP 72 | 12:01 AM | *L. A. Passenger* | AT 70 | 12:30 AM | *San Diego Local* |
| SP 56 | 6:00 AM | *Tehachapi* | SP 71 | 6:00 AM | *S. F. Passenger* |
| SP 5 | 7:00 AM | *Argonaut* | AT 72 | 8:00 AM | *San Diegan* |
| SP 43 | 7:10 AM | *Californian* | SP 99 | 8:15 AM | *Morning Daylight* |
| UP 37 | 7:15 AM | *Pony Express* | SP 51 | 8:25 AM | *San Joaquin Daylight* |
| AT 1 | 7:15 AM | *Scout* | UP 4 | 9:30 AM | *Utahn* |
| AT 21 | 7:30 AM | *El Capitan* | AT 42 | 10:10 AM | *Motor* |
| AT 3 | 7:45 AM | *California Limited* | AT 74 | 11:45 AM | *San Diegan* |
| SP 70 | 8:00 AM | *Coaster* | UP 2 | 12:01 PM | *Los Angeles Limited* |
| AT 19 | 8:30 AM | *Chief* | SP 97 | 12:15 PM | *Noon Daylight* |
| AT 17 | 8:45 AM | *Super Chief* | SP 4 | 12:30 PM | *Golden State* |
| SP 60 | 8:45 AM | *West Coast* | AT 20 | 12:30 PM | *Chief* |
| SP 76 | 9:00 AM | *Lark* | SP 2 | 12:45 PM | *Sunset Limited* |
| UP 103 | 9:00 AM | *City of Los Angeles* | AT 22 | 1:30 PM | *El Capitan* |
| SP 58 | 9:10 AM | *Owl* | AT 24 | 1:30 PM | *Grand Canyon* |
| AT 51 | 9:20 AM | *Motor* | SP 40 | 2:45 PM | *Imperial* |
| SP 1 | 9:25 AM | *Sunset Limited* | AT 76 | 3:30 PM | *San Diegan* |
| SP 47 | 9:45 AM | *Mail and Express* | UP 104 | 5:00 PM | *City of Los Angeles* |
| UP 1 | 10:40 AM | *Los Angeles Limited* | AT 54 | 5:30 PM | *Motor* |
| AT 23 | 10:40 AM | *Grand Canyon* | SP 57 | 5:50 PM | *Owl* |
| AT 71 | 10:45 AM | *San Diegan* | SP 48 | 6:00 PM | *Mail and Express* |
| SP 39 | 2:00 PM | *Imperial* | UP 38 | 6:00 PM | *Pony Express* |
| AT 73 | 2:30 PM | *San Diegan* | AT 4 | 7:00 PM | *California Limited* |
| UP 3 | 4:00 PM | *Utahn* | AT 78 | 7:30 PM | *San Diegan* |
| AT 53 | 4:00 PM | *Motor* | SP 59 | 7:30 PM | *West Coast* |
| SP 3 | 5:15 PM | *Golden State* | SP 69 | 7:55 PM | *Coaster* |
| AT 75 | 6:00 PM | *San Diego Local* | AT 18 | 8:00 PM | *Super Chief* |
| SP 98 | 6:00 PM | *Morning Daylight* | SP 44 | 8:10 PM | *Californian* |
| AT 77 | 6:30 PM | *San Diegan* | AT 2 | 8:15 PM | *Scout* |
| SP 52 | 7:50 PM | *San Joaquin Daylight* | SP 6 | 8:30 PM | *Argonaut* |
| AT 7 | 8:00 PM | *Mail and Express* | SP 55 | 8:30 PM | *Tehachapi* |
| SP 96 | 9:55 PM | *Noon Daylight* | SP 75 | 9:00 PM | *Lark* |
| AT 79 | 10:00 PM | *San Diegan* | AT 8 | 11:30 PM | *Mail and Express* |

entranceway, to the newsstand. Early morning editions of the *Times* and the *Examiner* are already stacked chin high, but melt down rapidly as newspapers and nickels are swapped to the tune of ringing cash registers. The first editions of the *Herald-Express* and the tabloid *Daily News,* with its peach-colored newsprint and racy headlines, have arrived, too, and sell about as quickly as the more serious morning papers.

More people. The front doors never find time to swing shut. Autos have jammed up in the parking lot, the taxis are jockeying for position and the early morning Red Cars from Pasadena and El Monte have pulled up out on Aliso Street with more customers for LAUPT. But the biggest crowds are about to descend from the train platforms, as the hour between 7 and 8 witnesses the arrival of no less than six trains: SP 5, the *Argonaut,* pulls in from New Orleans at 7 sharp; the *Californian* (SP 43), bearing cars that originated in Memphis and followed the Rock Island line across Arkansas, Oklahoma and the panhandle of Texas to join the SP line at Tucumcari, N.M., arrives at 7:10; Union Pacific 37, the *Pony Express,* eases in only five minutes later, at 7:15 just at the same time the Santa Fe's train 1, the *Scout,* appears a few platforms away.

Passengers from both trains vie for walking space as they flood down the ramp to the pedestrian tunnel. The *Pony Express* has a light crowd today, however; it's primarily a mail train from Chicago with local stops but has through cars from Kansas City, Portland, Oregon, and even Butte, Montana. The *Scout* is a different story. It's an economy coach and tourist sleeper consist (the Pullmans feature budget-priced uppers and lowers) which takes the "southern" Santa Fe main line via Amarillo, and today it's bulging with humanity.

Within minutes, there's a stir on track 12; the Santa Fe's *El Capitan* is arriving. It pulls to a stop a minute or two behind its advertised arrival of 7:30, and disgorges another

6:55 a.m.
(Above) The *Argonaut,* SP No. 5 from El Paso, Houston and New Orleans, crosses the Los Angeles River for its 7:00 a.m. arrival at the station. **William D. Middleton**

7:15 a.m.
(Left) The *Pony Express,* Union Pacific train 37, arrives from Chicago. This photo was taken in May 1947, when many UP passenger trains still rated heavy steam power. **Stan Kistler**

big crowd of tourists. The "El Cap" is the Santa Fe's premier all-coach streamliner—and is running a full 16 cars today, everyone a lightweight, streamlined vehicle designed to lure the customers away from buses and their own cars. Of course, with World War II over only a little more than two years, it still isn't easy to get the new family auto of your choice, but the Santa Fe at least already realizes that the highways are to be its chief competitors for the traveller's dollar. The *El Cap* is deluxe in every way. While the *Scout* takes the Santa Fe line through Amarillo, the *El Capitan* arrives via La Junta and Albuquerque.

The Santa Fe is still star of the show 15 minutes later when Number 3, the *California Limited,* pulls in. It's another very long train today—18 heavyweight sleepers, coaches, diners and head-end cars. Also operating via Albuquerque, the *California Limited* was at one time a premier train but in the postwar era has been downgraded a bit to mainline workhorse. In addition to the usual Chicago to

**8:00 a.m.**
(Above) GS-4 steam locomotive 4444 brings in *The Coaster* from San Francisco.
***Donald Duke***

**8:15 a.m.**
(Right) The *Morning Daylight* pulls out of Track No. 8 for San Francisco. Its brilliant red, orange and silver-hued streamlined consist is headed up by Lima-built GS-4 4455. The station is in the background; the busy post office Terminal Annex is behind the smoke, with railway mail cars spotted on access tracks at right.
***Donald Duke***

Los Angeles Pullmans, it sports sleepers from Denver and Albuquerque, and one from Phoenix added at the Mojave Desert tank town of Cadiz.

At 8 a.m. Terminal Tower maneuvers the simultaneous arrival of Southern Pacific's train 70, the *Coaster,* the secondary overnight train from San Francisco, and departure of ATSF 72, the first *San Diegan* of the day. The streamlined *San Diegans* were, perhaps, the closest approach that Los Angeles ever had to "corridor" rail service (a term not yet invented in 1949); there were four per day in each direction, zipping off the 133 miles in two hours and 45 minutes. They were, ultimately, to become virtually the only LAUPT trains to thrive in the jet age.

Inside the station, the crowds grow thicker, the pace more frenetic. The lines at the ticket windows (separate groups for SP, UP and Santa Fe) are now quite long, with tempers here and there becoming a bit frayed as short-haul passengers get hung up behind a family of four booking a round trip to Maine. The thump of the dating machines is heard above the din, mingling with the sound of drawers being opened and closed as clerks search for the proper tickets, tariffs and timetables in an era innocent of electronic gadgetry in ticketing procedures.

"No, ma'am, there's just no space left on the *Daylight,* but I can get you a seat on the *San Joaquin* and you can take the ferry over from the Oakland Mole," one linen-jacketed clerk can be heard saying to a customer who is just about to miss both trains if she doesn't make up her mind. At the next wicket, a man in a cowboy hat is learning that the 12:01 p.m. *Los Angeles Limited* will get him into Salt Lake City at 6:10 a.m. the next day, but that there's plenty of sleeping-car space available, a club lounge car to relax in, and no extra fare. "Guess I'll take an upper, then," he says, and the Union Pacific (and the Pullman Company) have earned a few more dollars.

8:25 a.m.
The *San Joaquin Daylight* rates a double-header for its departure to San Francisco. Lots of mountain climbing is ahead, through Saugus, then over the Tehachapis to Bakersfield. **Donald Duke**

Sure enough, the sold-out *Morning Daylight*, SP train 99, leaves on the dot at 8:15 a.m., its Lima-built GS-4 4-8-4 steam locomotive pulling a full complement of 19 light-weight passenger cars in the famed "Daylight" orange, yellow and silver colors. Its graceful features framed by the station's Mediterranean clock tower, the train momentarily forms a complete tableau of transportation. Since its inauguration back in 1937, two years before the opening of LAUPT, this one train had often been referred to as the most beautiful train in the world. Fitting then, that its terminal be one of the most beautiful stations in the world. Handsome or not, no one could deny that the *Daylight* was successful; so often did it become sold out that the company had put on a second prestige LA-San Francisco day train—the *Noon Daylight*—back in 1940. It took the *Daylight* until 6 p.m. to reach San Francisco, but in 1948 nobody had heard of Pacific Southwest Airlines, jet flights were not leaving every hour on the hour for points north,

and the trackside scenery along miles and miles of the blue Pacific was incomparable. It was the way to go, and the SP had its hands full.

The lady who missed the *Daylight* could catch a very similar train in appearance—the *San Joaquin Daylight*, scheduled to leave just 10 minutes later at 8:25. Train 51 arrived Oakland Pier at 7:32 p.m., and a short, breezy ferryboat ride would land her in San Francisco in time for dinner at one of The City's famed dining spots. The *San Joaquin* went a different route—winding through the Tehachapi Mountains, around the famous "Loop," then down into Bakersfield and a fast ride straight up the center of the San Joaquin Valley, California's agricultural wonderland. If the scenery wasn't quite as spectacular, the on-board services were typically good, and that ride over the Loop *was* something to write home about.

Just as things over on the SP side are beginning to quiet down, Santa Fe personnel prepare for the arrivals just 15 minutes apart of two of that line's finest. Train 19, the *Chief*, was in at 8:30, followed at 8:45 by arrival of the flagship of the fleet, train 17, the *Super Chief*.

Each train has its fans. The *Chief* had been the Santa Fe's top train until the 1937 inauguration of the *Super*, but even in 1948 it carried its colors proudly, and offered through sleeping cars from New York and Washington, something the railroads had not been coaxed into until after the war's end. It was all streamlined, carried both coaches and Pullmans, and you had to fork over $10 extra fare to ride her. The *Super*, of course, was in a class by itself. No

8:45 a.m.
The *West Coast*, in from Portland via the San Joaquin Valley, rounds the sharp curve to this crossing over the Los Angeles River and Santa Fe's bankside tracks (foreground). Pulling the train is this unique Southern Pacific cab-forward steam locomotive.
**Donald Duke**

**9:00 a.m.**
The streamlined *City of Los Angeles,* Union Pacific train No. 103, arrives from Chicago, having made the trip in its scheduled 39¾ hours.
***Stan Kistler***

**9:20 a.m.**

(Below) Santa Fe's Electro-Motive rail car, arriving from San Bernardino, passes Mission Tower. Built by General Motors, this type of car was primarily used to carry baggage, express and the U.S. mail on local runs. Some room was available for passengers. ***Donald Duke***

**9:30 a.m.**

(Right) The *Utahn,* UP No. 4, departs for Salt Lake City. Top photo shows the train on June 1, 1947, behind a mighty UP 4-8-4 steam locomotive with smoke deflectors. Bottom photo shows the train seven months later behind spanking new Electro-Motive F3 diesel units with a leased Santa Fe steam generator car to provide heat for the coaches. Locomotives of this type were usually assigned to freight trains.
***Both: Stan Kistler***

coach passengers were permitted. First class only—at a $15 extra fare. And the *Super Chief* was faster; although arrival in Los Angeles was only 15 minutes later than the *Chief,* it had left Chicago nearly six hours later, making the 2,224 miles in thirty-nine and three-quarter hours. The *Super* didn't tarry.

Terminal Tower also lined an 8:45 a.m. arrival for SP's train 60, the *West Coast,* an all-heavyweight coach, tourist and standard sleeper train from Portland via Sacramento. This influx of passengers from the Santa Fe and the SP was now straining the taxicabs, buses and streetcars outside, and not a few passengers were having to wait for things to quiet down a bit for a chance to get to a hotel or home. But there was much more to come, for the hour of 9 a.m. saw the arrival of two "glamor" trains—the SP's overnight *Lark* from San Francisco and Union Pacific's premier *City of Los Angeles.* To make matters even more complicated, these days the *Lark* (trains 75 and 76) was sometimes running in two—or even three—sections about 10 minutes apart. And if the *City* was on time (and the UP tried its best), those few minutes prior to 9 a.m. were frequently enough to give the towerman a few gray hairs.

The *Lark* was another all-Pullman train. The business traffic between California's two biggest cities always was heavy, and in 1948 the overnight train was considered the ideal way to have a full day free for conferences and business activity. Thirty years later, that would still be the custom in Europe, though not in the U.S. And the SP pampered its *Lark* passengers with a lounge car and a triple-unit diner.

As for UP's *City of Los Angeles,* train 103, it was already a legend even though its scenic dome cars were still in the future. Always spotless both inside and out, neatly turned out in UP's regulation yellow with red and black trim, the *City* was but one of a fleet of similarly named trains also serving San Francisco, Portland and Denver and all travel-ing east to Omaha and Chicago. It did carry coach passengers, but its Pullmans were all-room cars and the timetable promised "barber, valet, bath and radio." On the way from Chicago, train 103 served Omaha, Cheyenne, Salt Lake City and Las Vegas. In 1948, Las Vegas still wasn't the terrific entertainment and gambling magnet it was to become later, but the UP was already noting a steady upswing in passenger activity there.

Swiftly, the incoming trains were emptied to allow the switching locomotives of the three railroads (LAUPT did not, like some other union stations, employ its own equipment in making up or dismantling trains) to pull the consists back to the coach yards, clearing the 16 passenger loading tracks for more trains to come. And another came almost immediately on the heels of the *Lark* and the *City;* SP train 58, the *Owl,* a heavyweight coach and sleeper consist from Oakland via Los Banos and the San Joaquin Valley. Ten minutes after that, here comes ATSF train 51, the

*San Bernardino Local* via Fullerton. This train, shown on the timetable as a motor (a self-propelled railcar), often was in actuality a three-car train hauled by a steam locomotive.

Almost unnoticed in the hubbub, the SP's *Sunset Limited* arrives at 9:25. The *Sunset* (train 1) was the Southern Pacific's best coach and sleeper train from New Orleans via Houston, San Antonio and El Paso. In 1948 it has yet to be upgraded to a streamliner, but new equipment is on order. At 9:30 a.m., UP's *Utahn* departs. It is a coach and sleeper consist to Omaha, with heavyweight and lightweight streamlined cars intermixed. Through cars are handled to St. Louis. The *Utahn*, train 4, is not exactly the Ritz, but on the UP even the second string isn't so bad. The station's train announcer barely has time to catch his breath before proclaiming the arrival of SP train 47, the *Mail & Express*, from El Paso. But few take much notice; number 47 is primarily a "head end" train with only a single accommodation coach for riders in no particular hurry.

The 10 o'clock hour brings only four movements, and the terminal is settling down to the more relaxed pace which will carry it through the middle of the day. First is the departure of Santa Fe motor 42 to San Bernardino via Pasadena, at 10:10. A handful of passengers climb the ramp to board the Santa Fe's Electro-Motive-built motor car. Thirty minutes later heralds the arrival of both Union Pacific's train 1, the *Los Angeles Limited,* a coach and sleeper from Chicago, and the Santa Fe's train 23, the *Grand Canyon*. This train, operating via Amarillo, often has a second section, particularly in the summer, but today its 3700-class 4-8-4 steam locomotive carries no green flags for a following section, so there will be only about a dozen coaches and Pullmans for the yard crews to worry about. Rounding out the hour, five minutes later at 10:45, is arrival of the first Santa Fe *San Diegan* of the day. At 11:45 a.m., this train will depart for San Diego, giving railroad crews only an hour to clean and restock her. This turn-

**10:45 a.m.**
Santa Fe Train No. 71, the *San Diegan*, heads into the station. This steam locomotive and its rake of old, heavyweight passenger cars were originally used on the *Valley Flyer*, a San Joaquin Valley train. When this picture was taken, they had been "streamlined" with some metal and a paint job.
**Donald Duke**

**12:00 noon**
Passengers board Southern Pacific's *Noon Daylight* (far left), while a crewman climbs up the front of Santa Fe steamer 3782 for a final adjustment before the 12:30 departure of the *Chief*. Tracks 1 and 2 (right) were primarily used for the loading and unloading of express and parcels. **Donald Duke**

**12:01 p.m.**
(Below) The *Los Angeles Limited*, pulled by this unusual Fairbanks-Morse diesel locomotive, heads for Omaha and Chicago. **Stan Kistler**

**12:30 p.m.**
Two trains leave simultaneously for Chicago. SP's *Golden State* (left)
will go through Yuma, Phoenix and Tucumcari, while Santa Fe's *Chief*
will go through Flagstaff, Gallup and Albuquerque, before heading
north through Kansas City. This photo was taken from Mission Tower
on July 24, 1949, during the heyday of the long streamliner.
**William D. Middleton**

around of the *San Diegan* is, in fact, the only train activity until one minute past noon, giving terminal personnel a bit of a breather. They will need it.

THE NOON HOUR finds Union Station once again in high gear. The Fred Harvey grill and the snack shops are jammed. Veteran station employes—and not a few regular customers—head instead across Alameda Street for Felipe's, that longtime Los Angeles gastronomical institution where giant sandwiches and coffee and pie are dispensed on an assembly-line basis to eager crowds all day long, or to the little Mexican cafes along Olvera Street, across the Plaza. But for many others, the push is in the other direction, to the tracks where five major trains await departure, their diners already open for business.

Because railroad timetables traditionally omit the even noon and midnight hours, the first departure, that of Union Pacific's number 2, the *Los Angeles Limited,* is carded for 12:01 p.m. The *Limited,* despite its name, will not be in Chicago until 2 p.m. day after tomorrow, but many of its passengers are bound for intermediate points. The crowd getting on today is sparce, but many of its presently empty seats and berths will be taken by passengers getting on at the Union Pacific's East Los Angeles station, 24 minutes away by rail. There, UP feeder buses from Long Beach and Orange County points will meet the train; the UP has been a pioneer in this kind of intermodal transportation, touted as just the thing for auto-oriented Los Angeles.

On a nearby track rests another long orange, red and silver Southern Pacific streamliner, the *Noon Daylight.* It pulls out at 12:15 for San Francisco, a near-duplicate of its early-morning version. Two long-distance coach and sleeper

12:35 p.m.
(Right) The *Golden State Limited* crosses the Los Angeles River on the first leg of its journey.
**William D. Middleton**

trains leave at 12:30, Santa Fe's number 20, the *Chief,* and Southern Pacific's number 4, the *Golden State.* Recently streamlined, the *Golden State* offers another path to Chicago and the East—via Yuma, Phoenix, El Paso, Tucumcari, and the Rock Island to Kansas City and Chicago. This so-called "Golden State Route" has always been a longer, somewhat less spectacular alternate to the Santa Fe and the Union Pacific routes to the Windy City, but the SP and RI have made the most of it and kept the service up to snuff. And today's crowd of passengers for number 4 proves that the SP has been working at it. In fact, an extra fare is charged and the train now offers a through Pullman to New York via the Pennsylvania Railroad. SP train 2, the eastbound *Sunset Limited,* leaves at 12:45 p.m. and will follow in the wake of the *Golden State* all the way to El Paso.

It's the Santa Fe's show at 1:30 p.m., when it dispatches two major trains eastbound at the same moment. Departing then are trains 22, the *El Capitan,* and 24, the *Grand Canyon,* both for Chicago. This seeming duplication of schedule is explained by the fact that the all-coach *El Cap* will leave town via Pasadena and the second subdivision, while the more leisurely *Grand Canyon* with its heavyweight coach and sleeper consist will travel the third subdivision via Fullerton and Riverside. The two lines rejoin at San Bernardino, but the *El Cap* will beat the *Grand Canyon* to "San Berdoo" by a good 20 minutes, and be in Chicago a full eight hours sooner!

At 2 p.m. the SP's *Imperial,* train 39, makes its appearance, and another *San Diegan* rolls in at 2:30. At 2:45 the eastbound *Imperial,* train 40, leaves (with a different set of equipment than the westbound which has just arrived) and

12:45 p.m.
Southern Pacific No. 2, the *Sunset,*
heads for New Orleans.
**William D. Middleton**

1:30 p.m.
The *Grand Canyon* prepares to depart,
while diminutive Santa Fe switcher 611 putters
around with a cut of cars (far right). **Donald Duke**

sets out for Chicago by way of an interesting variation on the "Golden State" route; it dips down through the center of California's sub-sea level Imperial Valley (hence its name), passes through a little slice of northern Mexico, reenters the U.S. west of Yuma, Arizona, and then serves as the secondary "slow" train to Chicago on the SP-Rock Island route. This train also picks up a through sleeper from San Diego at El Centro which has traversed the scenic Carrizo Gorge route on the SP subsidiary San Diego & Arizona Eastern line.

There's a mini-lull now, with only the 3:30 departure of another *San Diegan* (train 76) and the twin 4 p.m. arrivals of UP 3, the *Utahn,* and the Santa Fe motor (train 53) from San Bernardino via Fullerton.

The five o'clock hour at LAUPT finds things pretty tame compared to, say, Grand Central or Penn Station in New York due to the total absence of any commuter trains. But you wouldn't realize that just before 5 p.m., judging from the mob of passengers rushing toward the Union Pacific's *City of Los Angeles,* carded out of the station on its eastbound voyage to Chicago precisely at 5:00. The passengers are finally checked in, and the *City* sails away a bit tardy today, just before the 5:15 arrival of SP train 3, the *Golden State.* At 5:30 another Santa Fe *motor,* making local stops to San Bernardino via Fullerton (train 54) leaves the terminal. Is this a "commuter" train? Not really; it attracts few passengers these days and the Santa Fe would like to get rid of it.

At 5:50 p.m. SP train 57, the *Owl,* leaves for Oakland Pier via the San Joaquin Valley. It's the first "overnight" train to the Bay Area, and carries Pullman cars and a diner.

1:30 p.m.
The *El Capitan,* Santa Fe's all-coach streamliner, heads for Kansas City and Chicago. **William D. Middleton**

**2:00 p.m.**
(Above) Arriving from Calexico, SP's *Imperial* passes Terminal Tower.

**2:20 p.m.**
(Right) On Santa Fe's tracks, a *San Diegan*, pulled by this diesel locomotive, nears the approach to the station.

*Both: William D. Middleton*

Six o'clock must be a headache to the people who operate Terminal Tower, and to the station staff as well. At exactly that moment the timecard shows the arrival of two trains and the departure of two. And the thickening of the crowd of people pushing past each other in the narrow platform tunnel, fighting their way in both directions, proves the point. Heading out are SP 48, the *Mail & Express* to El Paso, ("local passengers only"), and UP 38, the *Pony Express* with through coaches and sleepers, and even a set-out Pullman for Las Vegas. Coming in are ATSF 75, the *San Diego Local* (the only "all stops" train on the route) and the SP *Morning Daylight*, train 98. Only the last-named train is in the carriage trade class.

*San Diegan* 77 arrives at 6:30, just as the final switching moves are made to ready the departure of four trains between 7 and 8 p.m. Right at 7:00 Santa Fe's train 4, the *California Limited*, leaves with its long string of heavy-weight coaches and Pullmans, followed by the 7:30 depar-

tures of *San Diegan* 78 and SP 59, the *West Coast* for Portland via the San Joaquin Valley. SP's *San Joaquin Daylight* (train 52) arrives at 7:50 p.m., and five minutes later, at 7:55, SP 69, the *Coaster*, leaves for San Francisco via the Coast route.

The crowd is thinning out now in the Harvey House. The barber shop is closing; there are fewer people standing near the entrance to the gift shop; and the patio and court-yard are now deserted, the chill February winds having driven even the hardiest souls inside to the steam-heated waiting room. It's even possible to make a telephone call without waiting for one of the 24 booths in the telephone annex off the main arcade. But there's a knot of people at the information booth, and not a few anxious glances at wristwatches as the hour ticks toward eight o'clock. What's happening down at the far end of the concourse? Looks like pandemonium down there, toward the tunnel to the plat-forms.

*William D. Middleton*

5:15 p.m.
Train crewmen saunter in front of Santa Fe diesel 311 at the north end of platform 5; the *Golden State* has pulled in from Chicago on track 4.

Closer examination reveals several lines of passengers trying to sort themselves out in front of the Pullman conductors' desks. The *Super Chief*, Santa Fe train 18, is due to leave at 8:00 and the lordly *Lark* for San Francisco at 9:00, and these trains, plus a few lesser ones, all have their Pullman conductors stationed at special stands in front of the train gates to facilitate orderly and expeditious boarding of the cars. The Pullman Company, one remembers, does not subject its sleeping-car passengers to having their tickets examined and lifted in the dead of night; no, indeed, one surrenders one's ticket before boarding and is assured of a journey undisturbed by officialdom. And the *Super Chief's* passengers are mighty particular folks. Many will not get on until the train stops at Pasadena—the hubbub and jostle of Union Station will not be for them.

The *Super* does indeed pull out promptly at 8:00, just as its even faster cousin, number 7, the *Mail & Express*, creeps in on a side track over toward the Terminal Annex. If one can set one's watch by the *Super Chief*, one can do likewise by number 7. "The mail must go through" is no idle dictum for the railroads in 1948, and that goes double for the Santa Fe with its double-track, high-speed main line all the way to Chicago.

SP train 44, the *Californian*, leaves at 8:10, with sleepers for Memphis, Phoenix, Tucson and points east along the Golden State Route; ATSF train 2, the *Scout*, pulls out five minutes later on a slower schedule to Chicago. At 8:30 the SP dispatches both its number 6, the *Argonaut*, for New Orleans, and number 55, the *Tehachapi*, for Oakland Pier via the San Joaquin Valley, a slow, 22-hour, all-stops drag if ever there was one.

The *Lark*, SP train 75, is once again running in two sections tonight. The first, streamlined, carries only sleepers, lounge and dining cars. But so brisk is demand for transportation to the Bay Area that mere coach passengers are permitted aboard the second section. The *Lark* leaves on the dot, the second section following its rear markers by 10 minutes. Both will stop at the SP's stucco Glendale station for additional passengers.

Arriving at 9:55 p.m. is SP's *Noon Daylight*, train 96. It left San Francisco's Third and Townsend Street Station at 12:15 p.m. and stopped at only the principal stations, including San Jose, San Luis Obispo and Santa Barbara. With the *Noon Daylight's* passengers dispersed to their ultimate destinations, Union Station is quiet. Only the 10 p.m. arrival of the last *San Diegan* of the day, Santa Fe 79, breaks the stillness. The 11:30 p.m. departure of the Santa Fe's train 8, the *Mail & Express*, will hardly affect LAUPT itself, and another busy day of catering to the traveling multitudes is over. Glancing up at the floodlit clock tower, its hands pointing to midnight, the Assistant Terminal Superintendent trudges toward his car, his day's duties finished. February 29 will not come along for another four years, but another 66 trains, another tens of thousands of passengers, another million details, will come again tomorrow. Los Angeles Union Station will be ready.

5:30 p.m.
Santa Fe's *San Bernardino Local* leaves the station.
**Donald Duke**

(Above) LOS ANGELES CITY HALL is faintly visible through the smog in this view taken on October 8, 1955, from the south end of the station's tracks. Southern Pacific's train 94, the *Starlight*, has just arrived from San Francisco behind this red and orange Alco PA diesel. The observation car behind the engine belongs to the *San Joaquin Daylight*. Railway Express Agency trucks await loading space at left. **William D. Middleton**

(Left) Santa Fe's era of steam locomotives came to an end with the departure of No. 3759 on February 6, 1955. **Stan Kistler**

(Above) THIS PAIR of Budd RDC (Rail Diesel Car) self-propelled units served the Santa Fe's San Diego service during a portion of the 1950s.

(Above, right) SWITCHING CHORES, shared by the three railroads, shifted to diesel power in the 1950s. A Union Pacific locomotive tows a Pullman car over the Vignes bridge (view from Terminal Tower).

(Right) DOME CARS and lightweight streamliners appeared in the Fifties as the trains were modernized to compete with the trend toward automobiles and airplanes.

***ALL: Donald Duke***

(Left) THE STREAMLINED LUXURY of Union Pacific's *Challenger* (at left) was still packing them in during the 1950s.
**Donald Duke**

(Below) THE LEAD UNIT of a brace of diesel locomotives passes Mission Tower a minute past 2 p.m. in May 1954 as the *Challenger* approaches the Los Angeles River crossing on its way toward Chicago.
**William D. Middleton**

# *Chapter 3*

# CREATING THE NEW GATEWAY

THE IDEA of a union station for Los Angeles was not something that sprang up only a few years before any ground was broken. Rather, it was a long-standing civic dream that took almost three decades of struggle to realize.

It was a classic political confrontation with a determined government on one side and cost-conscious private enterprise on the other. Unlike today's airline terminals which are built with public funds, train stations of the past were paid for by the railroads using them. And so it was expected that the three transcontinental railroads serving Los Angeles would not only comply with the city's wishes but pay the costs as well. This they resisted, and what resulted was a long and complicated legal battle that was unprecedented in the city's history.

A MAJOR FACTOR in the Union Station battle was the location. The city insisted that it be built here, on what was known as the "Plaza site," adjacent to where the city was founded. In 1932, the area still a part of the city's Chinatown. *California Historical Society/Title Insurance & Trust Co. (L.A.)*

(Above) BEFORE UNION STATION went into service, trains passed along Alameda St. on their way to Southern Pacific's Central Station. The traffic congestion that this caused was one reason why the city and the railroad commission called for grade separation and a new station at the Plaza. Southern Pacific's suggested answer to this problem was to reroute the trains across the Los Angeles River, and connect them by elevated tracks to the station. Seen here on Alameda at Second St. is Southern Pacific's *Lark*, arriving from San Francisco, about 1938. **Stan Kistler**

# The Case for a Station

The story begins two decades before the great station took shape. In July 1915 several city agencies seeking the removal of grade crossings and improved transportation facilities filed a complaint with the California Railroad Commission against the Santa Fe, Los Angeles and Salt Lake (later the Union Pacific) and Southern Pacific Railroads. For the first time, the issue of consolidation of certain duplicate facilities—including terminals—arose.

As a harbinger of what was to come later, an immediate disagreement arose between the city and the railroad commission over who had jurisdiction over what. While it was agreed that the commission had jurisdiction over the establishment of a union station, each party—the city and

the commission—maintained that it had jurisdiction over grade crossings. The matter was decided on June 11, 1917, when the California Supreme Court declared that all jurisdiction was in the hands of the commission.

With that accomplished, the railroad commission then set out to examine the situation and prepare a comprehensive report.

Among its findings were the following arguments in favor of a union station:

1. The three railroads were close enough so that connection would be simple. Only some short connecting track would be required.
2. The existing depots for the Santa Fe and Los Angeles and Salt Lake Railroads were inadequate.
3. The majority of local residents wanted a new station.
4. There would be increased convenience to passengers.
5. Certain operating expenses of the railroads would be reduced by establishing a common facility.
6. It would simplify the highly important matter of grade separations.
7. It would create the opportunity to find an efficient location with respect to transit lines and the business center, and yet be close to the coach yard and mechanical facilities.
8. It would add advertising value by creating a good impression on visitors.

The report went on to discuss possible sites for such a station. In favor of a union station at the Plaza, the report listed these arguments:

1. The site was at the converging point of many streets and was near the end of principal business streets.
2. More streetcar lines reached this location than anywhere else.
3. It was near a point which would probably be the northerly end of the first subway to be built in Los Angeles. (Considered the most important argument.)

4. It was convenient to coach and shop yards.
5. The entire project could be at ground level, with no elevated track.
6. It allowed room for more railroads to enter Los Angeles.
7. It would tend to stabilize values in the downtown district.

Some of these arguments were direct rebuttals against anti-union station sentiment. The fifth one, for instance, was directed against Southern Pacific's plan for elevated track into its Central Station as a way of relieving grade crossings. The sixth argument was directed to the belief that the railroads were resisting a union station so that they could maintain a monopoly on the area, and keep other lines from entering.

Not surprisingly, the report's recommendations were challenged by the railroad's engineers, who cited these reasons against a station at the Plaza:

1. Politics. The plan was inconsistent with the railroads' own wishes.
2. The cost. Not only would a completely new building have to be constructed, but most of the land would have to be acquired from private owners.
3. Until the subway was built, there would be no benefit to present commutation service of the Pacific Electric.
4. It would have to be a stub-end depot—a decided operational disadvantage.
5. Several streets would have to be crossed at different grades.

Finally, on April 26, 1921, after a series of conferences in which both sides aired their differences, the Commission gave its order: The three railroads and Pacific Electric (the region's major electric interurban carrier) were to start at once on a new depot at the Plaza, and grade crossings on Alameda, Macy, Seventh and Aliso streets were to be eliminated. Furthermore, the railroads were to name a joint committee in 30 days and file plans within six months.

The results? Not one aspect of the order was carried through. Instead, the whole idea was met with years of resistance, doubt and delay.

The railroads retaliated by appealing first to the Commission, and then to the California Supreme Court. The first brought a rehearing and only one modification: Pacific Electric was dropped from the order. The second brought a more significant decision: the court cancelled the order and ruled that the railroad commission had no power to order railroads to build a union station or to remove grade crossings.

A later appeal to the United States Supreme Court brought the same decision.

The city and the railroads took their cases before the Interstate Commerce Commission in 1923. The ICC considered both plans, but decided that it lacked the necessary jurisdiction. It did, however, find the city's plan for a union station at the Plaza to be more in the public interest.

ALTHOUGH it is hard to say just how ardently the railroads wanted *any* kind of a union station, at least the SP's idea of elevating its venerable Central Station, located on Central Avenue just north of Sixth, would have incorporated significant improvement in commuter travel, much of which was provided by the SP's subsidiary Pacific Electric.

The plan actually started with the PE, which, in 1925, had opened the city's first real rapid transit line—the mile-long subway from Glendale Blvd. and Beverly Blvd. under Bunker Hill to a new underground terminal at Fifth and Hill streets. This had speeded Glendale, Burbank and Hollywood cars considerably, and set off a new clamor for Los Angeles to have the kind of rail rapid transit enjoyed by some of the major Eastern cities.

The city, naturally, wanted more subways but PE officials felt that, if any structures were to be built, they would have to be elevated because of the staggering cost of tunneling—even in those pre-inflationary days. And so their thoughts turned to a speedier entrance into downtown for

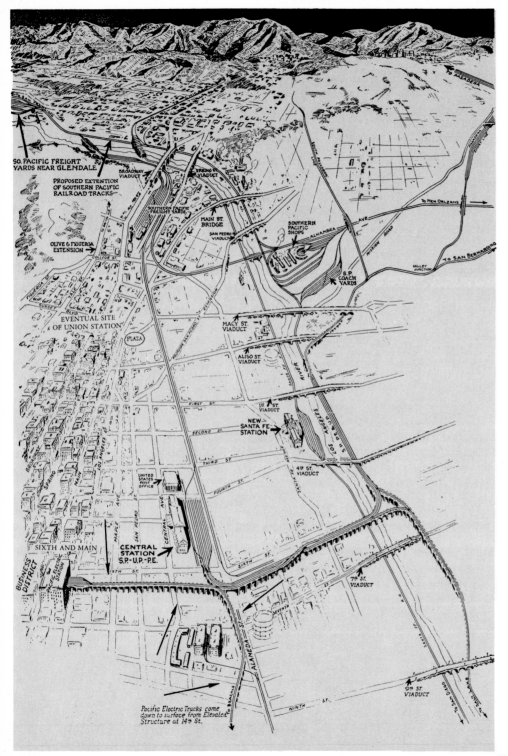

So. Pacific Freight Yards near Glendale

Proposed Extention of Southern Pacific Railroad Tracks

Olive & Figueroa Extension

Broadway Viaduct

Spring St Viaduct

Southern Pacific Freight Yards

Main St Bridge

San Pedro Viaduct

Southern Pacific Shops

S.P. Coach Yards

To New Orleans

To San Bernardino

Valley Junction

College St.

Eventual Site of Union Station

Plaza

Macy St. Viaduct

Aliso St. Viaduct

First St. Viaduct

1st St Viaduct

New Santa Fe Station

Second St.

Third St.

4th St. Viaduct

Fourth St.

United States Post Office

Central Station S.P.-U.P.-P.E.

Sixth And Main

Business District

7th St. Viaduct

9th St. Viaduct

Ninth St.

Pacific Electric Tracks come down to surface from Elevated Structure at 14th St.

the Long Beach and Pasadena rail lines, even then some of PE's heaviest.

Early in 1926 PE and SP proposed an elevated structure which would benefit both the PE's Big Red Cars and the SP's long-distance trains, which were forced to run the gauntlet of nearly a mile and a half along the middle of congested Alameda Street. The sight of long, heavy passenger trains inching their way along that truck-clogged thoroughfare had long infuriated city and railroad officials alike.

PE already had a short elevated stretch of trackage from its principal Sixth and Main street station, east to San Pedro Street, less than one-third of a mile. There, the Red Cars turned either north to Pasadena and points east, or south to Long Beach and the Harbor area. In either case, long stretches of street running were required, and, especially during rush hours, travel was slow.

The idea was to extend this elevated viaduct for PE trains further east, all the way to Alameda Street, another half mile. At this point the PE's elevated tracks would intersect with SP mainline tracks, also elevated, but curving north into the grounds of Central Station. The PE and SP trains would share trackage as the elevated structure continued eastward, crossing the Los Angeles River. On the east bank the lines would divide; a curve to the south would permit trains of the Union Pacific to diverge to their own tracks, while SP and PE trains would swing north to follow the river to a point north of First Street.

Here would be another junction; PE's electrified tracks would turn east, to join the old Macy Street alignment near the PE's sprawling Macy Shops. SP tracks, on the other hand, would continue north along the river to join their old alignment near what is now Taylor freightyard.

SOUTHERN PACIFIC AND PACIFIC ELECTRIC proposed this grand plan in the 1920s to elevate the tracks into Central Station (serving Southern Pacific and Union Pacific trains) and extend the Pacific Electric elevated out of its Sixth and Main depot to tie in with the mainline trackage.

Finally, PE's busy Long Beach, San Pedro and Santa Ana trains would leave the elevated structure just opposite Central Station, swinging southward to join the four-track right-of-way at Ninth Street.

This complex of elevated tracks would have cost $25 million, but would have benefited both PE and SP, and brought the city its first extensive rapid transit improvements aside from the Hollywood subway. PE General Manager David W. Pontius emphasized that the PE could never afford such an elaborate improvement on its own, but if combined with plans for a union station, could be justified economically by the rail companies.

Actually, the plan would not have amounted to a "union" station. The Santa Fe was excluded. Its ancient La Grande Station, on the west bank of the Los Angeles River at Second and Santa Fe streets, would have continued in use due to lack of a feasible connection with the SP's elevateds. The UP, however, *was* included since its few transcontinental trains could easily be accommodated by the construction of just one curve east of the river.

The proposal for a network of elevated lines touched off one of the fiercest political battles in Los Angeles history. With its legal options running out, the city decided to take the case for a union station to the people. Two propositions were placed on the 1926 ballot. The first asked if a union station should be built, and the second asked specifically if it should be built at the Plaza.

The resulting campaign polarized the city as few issues ever had. Arrayed on one side—the side favoring the Central Station site and the elevated network—were the railroads and four of the city's six daily newspapers. On the other side stood the city and Harry Chandler's *Los Angeles Times.*

---

(Right) THIS APPEARED in *The Public Voice,* a "newspaper" sponsored by the railroads who opposed the stand of the *Los Angeles Times* on the subject of a Union Station at the Plaza. Although strictly propaganda, it failed to sway the public's vote. **Ralph Melching**

The city accused the railroads of wanting no station at all. The elevated scheme was pictured as a stall, a ruse, or, even worse, a potential property-value-destroying blight if the railroads were serious after all. The *Times* was suspected of plumping for a Plaza site because of Chandler's real estate investments. The campaign was acrimonious, with editorial cartoons depicting the city asleep at the switch while grasping railroad barons switched the city's future progress onto a rickety, unsafe, unsightly steel elevated structure. Editorial writers ridiculed the idea of the Big Red Cars riding high in the air; the future, they said, lay in underground subways which would logically converge on the Plaza union station site.

The PE's Pontius answered that the elevateds would "remove 1,200 trains daily from the streets and eliminate 18,000 grade crossings daily." Seven to 20 minutes would be cut from average commuting times, he added. It was not long before the union station plan became hopelessly tangled in the elevated issue and, prior to the May 2 referendum, it became clear that the *Times* and its allies had succeeded in alarming the public about the potential menace of steel juggernauts in the sky.

Proposition Number 8, favored by the PE-SP forces, actually did not pin down any site for the proposed union station, although the Central Station site was implicit in the accompanying master plan. Proposition Number 9 pegged the site squarely at the Plaza, and seemed to be the most clear-cut of the options.

Proposition 8, permitting "el" construction, was defeated soundly, 115,493 to 72,714. Proposition 9, for the Plaza union station, passed narrowly, 94,404 to 90,464. Angelenos had voted down rapid transit—at least in the form of an elevated system. They had approved, however narrowly, the idea of a union station at the Plaza. A milestone had been passed, and the city had scored an important victory.

BUT THE FIGHT was far from over, as the city was soon to learn. Once again the California Railroad Commission reviewed the situation, and in 1927 rendered its *second* order compelling the railroads to build the station. The commission acted in the belief that its order would be carried out just as soon as it was approved by the ICC.

That body, finding the station "warranted by public convenience and necessity," duly issued the necessary certificates for track extensions and construction.

The railroads replied by appealing *again* to the California Supreme Court, hoping to stall the project indefinitely. The city's reaction was prompt: a petition to a U.S. district court for a ruling compelling the ICC to hear further evidence in the city's favor.

In Los Angeles' view, the ICC was dragging its feet. What the city hoped to do was force that body to not only *permit* construction of a new terminal, but to *compel* it. Nothing less, the city felt, would get the railroads off dead center.

No sooner did the U.S. District Court in Washington, D.C., begin hearing the case, however, than the city of Los Angeles suddenly switched tactics—it demanded that the U.S. Court of Appeals take jurisdiction at once to speed resolution of the bitterly fought and thorny issue. Railroad attorneys were caught off guard, and the move (considered "brilliant" by the *Los Angeles Times*) paid off. After less than an hour's deliberation, the court moved the case up to the U.S. Court of Appeals.

Sure enough, the city's hunch was right. On February 25, 1929, the U.S. Court of Appeals ruled that the ICC did indeed have the authority to order construction of union stations, a precedent-setting decision which reversed positions long held by both the ICC and the railroads. Up to then, it had been thought the ICC's jurisdiction covered only track extensions, abandonments and the like.

The city's elation over this new turn of events was short-lived. The ICC, unhappy over being handed this unwanted mandate, appealed to the Supreme Court which overturned the appeals court's decision. The ICC couldn't force the building of union stations after all.

THIS AERIAL PHOTO shows a drawing of the proposed Union Station superimposed on the actual site. Shown in the vicinity are: (1) tracks at the throat of the yard; (2) Macy St.; (3) Aliso St.; (4) Alameda St.; (5) historic buildings; (6) Los Angeles St.; (7) The Plaza; (8) North Main St. It is interesting to note that Aliso St., which was then the route of Pacific Electric red cars to the north and east, has since been replaced by the Santa Ana Freeway. Also, the area just below and to the left of Macy St. is where the Terminal Annex post office was built. Finally, nearly all of the buildings in the top half of the picture have since been razed. *L.A.U.P.T.*

Or could it? The issue soon wound its way back to the California Supreme Court, which, after more hearings, upheld the Railroad Commission's original 1927 order directing construction of the station. This perforce started a new round of appeals, and, when the railroads took the case back to the U.S. Supreme Court, a bewildered *Los Angeles Times* wondered in print if the matter would ultimately be taken to the League of Nations, or even perhaps to Mussolini.

Finally, Los Angeles got the news it was longing for. After all the legal angles were played out, all the arguments heard, all the appeals exhausted, the nation's highest court on May 18, 1931, paved the way once and for all for Los Angeles' new union station.

The U.S. Supreme Court upheld the California Supreme Court, thus putting into full effect that body's backing of the Railroad Commission's mandate for a union station. It was now left for the railroads to act, and to act they had to come up with a plan.

Discussions started on design proposals and cost estimates. But just as the project began to move forward, a new threat, this one economic rather than legal, appeared. The country was by now in the grip of the Great Depression, and in October of 1932 the railroads asked for a moratorium on the project due to plummeting passenger patronage.

The city was in no mood to give up now. Rejecting the request, Los Angeles demanded that the station go ahead as planned. Then the railroads submitted a plan for a terminal on North Broadway that would cost about $2 million less than the one at the Plaza. This, too, was rejected. It was another stalemate.

Finally the Mayor of Los Angeles, Frank Shaw, met with the presidents of the three railroads in search of a compromise. The result was that the city agreed to provide $1 mil-lion in funds for the preliminary street work. The City Council approved the plan, even though one councilman denounced it as a blatant donation to the railroads. Following this offer, the railroads dropped their opposition and agreed to go ahead with the project, prompting the *Los Angeles Times* to say: "The city will no longer suffer the embarrassment that comes to any good host who must usher his guests in through the side entrance or bring them in the back way." Then, as a formality to obtain final approval, the railroads applied to the California Railroad Commission for what had become known as the Plaza "setback plan."

Survey work for the new station began in the Fall of 1933. In the following year, the site was cleared and the first phases of construction were launched. But completion was delayed by yet another impasse—this time from the Post Office Department, concerning the location of its new Terminal Annex. The department had previously announced its intention to build a new structure, but had never come up with a specific proposal. This abruptly changed on June 23, 1935, when it announced its plan to build a five-story structure on the corner of Alameda Street *south* of Macy Street.

Both the railroads and the city responded with a vigorous protest, claiming that the building would use up land allocated for the station, that its height would contrast unfavorably with the station's low profile, and that its location would worsen traffic congestion in the area. The railroads refused to deed the land, but when the government went ahead with condemnation proceedings anyway, they called a halt to the station's construction.

Several months later, the Post Office Department and the Treasury Department submitted a different proposal calling for a lower building that was to be located on a site *north* of Macy Street. Building of the station then resumed, and continued without delay until its opening.

THE FIRST OFFICIAL sketch of the Post Office was only tentative, but it showed the relation of the building to the station. A garden and a recessed arcade were proposed to connect the two structures. *Ralph Melching*

(Right) As a reaction against the government's proposal, a designer from the City Planning Commission submitted this drawing to illustrate how the Post Office would dwarf the station, if built. *Ralph Melching*

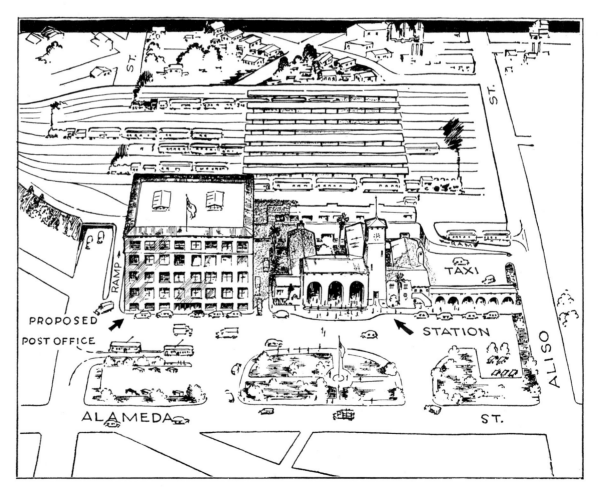

## Predecessors

WHEN LOS ANGELES was still the Old Pueblo, each railroad had its own station, a state of affairs that continued for many years. (Left) The San Pedro, Los Angeles and Salt Lake Railroad (later the Union Pacific) occupied this station, located on East First St., until 1924, when it was destroyed by fire. *Donald Duke*

TRAIN STATIONS generally preceded other development, and in 1892 there was still much open country around the abuilding Santa Fe La Grande Station (foreground) and the Salt Lake Station (behind it, to the left). *Donald Duke*

THE SANTA FE Railway occupied its La Grande Station for 46 years—longer than it was to be in residence at Union Station. Located on Santa Fe Avenue between First and Second streets, it was dedicated in 1893, and lasted until 1946 when it was torn down to make way for a freight terminal. The structure was originally distinguished by these Mosque-like domes, which were removed in 1933 as a result of the Long Beach earthquake. As a convenience to travelers, new hotels were opened up nearby, many of which continue today as part of L.A.'s skid row area. *Donald Duke*

(Top) THE LA GRANDE STATION, from the First Street Bridge looking south. *Donald Duke*

SOUTHERN PACIFIC operated out of three terminals before moving to Union Station. (Right) The first was little more than a storefront when the railroad took it over in 1884. Known as the River Station, it was later used for freight-yard offices and some local passenger service when the main business moved to the Arcade Depot (top two photos). Arcade, patterned after the road's "hometown" station in Sacramento, was opened in February 1888 and lasted until November 30, 1914, when the more elaborate Central Station was built on an adjoining site. After 1924, Central Station also served the Salt Lake Railroad. *All: Magna Collection*

When the California Railroad Commission prepared its report in 1919, it asked the railroads to find out how many passengers used their stations in an average day. The survey, taken in April 1918, yielded these results: Southern Pacific, 3,761; Santa Fe, 2,679; Salt Lake, 737.

THE BEGINNING . . . and the end of Central Station shows in these photos. When the SP terminal was completed in 1915 at a cost of $750,000, it was called the most expensive station west of Kansas City, and for the number of passengers handled, the most expensive in the United States. Not long after its opening, the Pacific Electric was still re-arranging its tracks in front (seen at left margin of photo). *Vernon J. Sappers Historical Collection*

(Below, left) This view, taken from the northeast in 1938, shows trainyard activity on most of the station's 10 tracks. *Melching Brothers*

(Below) By the early 1950s, the facade of the long-deserted edifice was peeling away. *Southern Pacific*

THE LOBBY of Central Station, circa 1915. *Vernon J. Sappers*

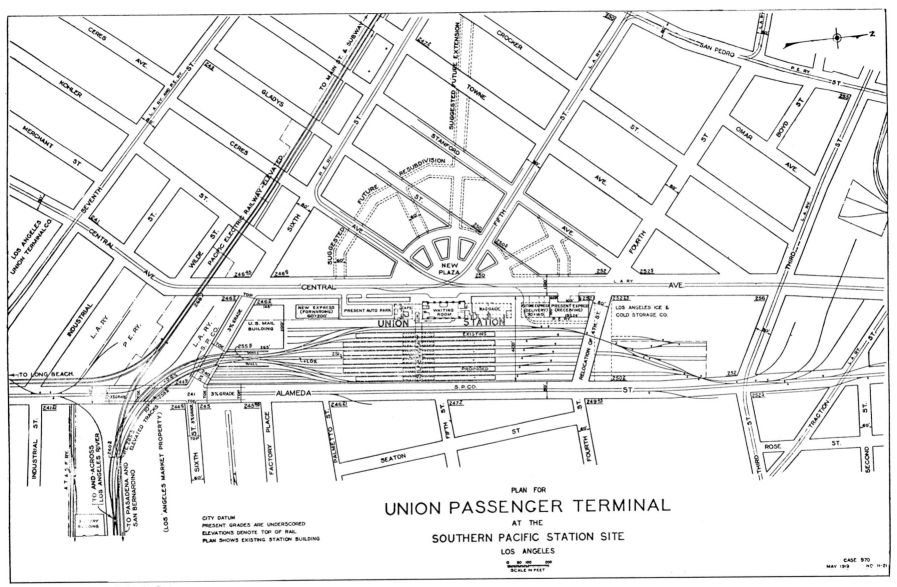

PLAN FOR

# UNION PASSENGER TERMINAL

AT THE

SOUTHERN PACIFIC STATION SITE

LOS ANGELES

CITY DATUM
PRESENT GRADES ARE UNDERSCORED
ELEVATIONS DENOTE TOP OF RAIL
PLAN SHOWS EXISTING STATION BUILDING

CASE 970
MAY 1919    NO 11-21

California Railroad Commission Engineering Dept.

A VARIETY OF SITES were considered for Union Station—many at existing stations. This plan, submitted by the Southern Pacific and Salt Lake railroads, made use of a facility already built and paid for. But its chief drawback, according to the California Railroad Commission, was that its space was limited for the required number of tracks and for future expansion. Also, many, including the Commission, were not in favor of the idea for elevated approaches into the station. And the two railroads refused to share the facility with the Santa Fe, excluding its use as a real Union Station. *Sherman Foundation Library*

THIS PLAN, submitted by the Santa Fe Railway, provided for a through instead of a stub-end terminal—which all of the lines preferred, and also allowed enough room for the desired number of tracks. The big disadvantage was that the terminal building itself was inadequate to meet the demands of increased service. Also, the city didn't like the setting—finding its warehouse district location too unsightly for a new railroad gateway. *Sherman Foundation Library*

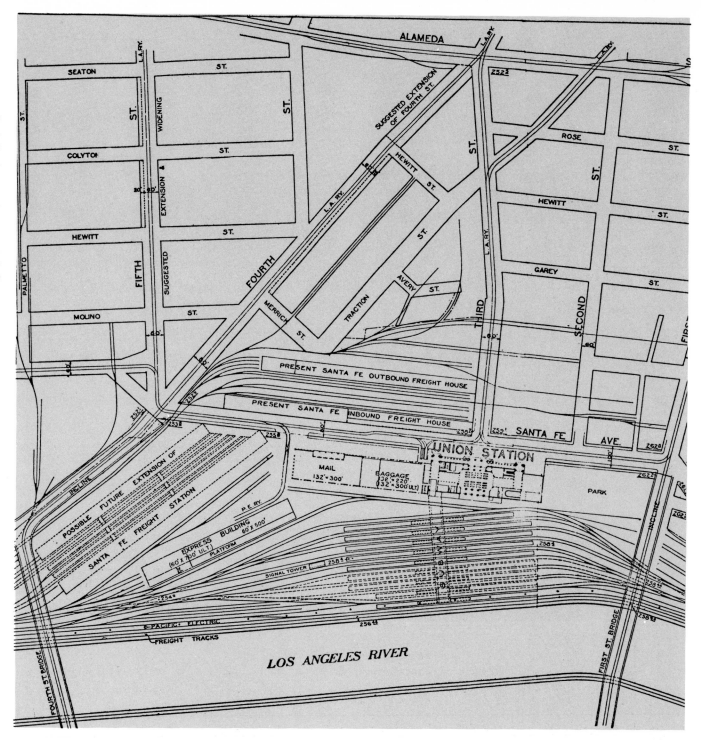

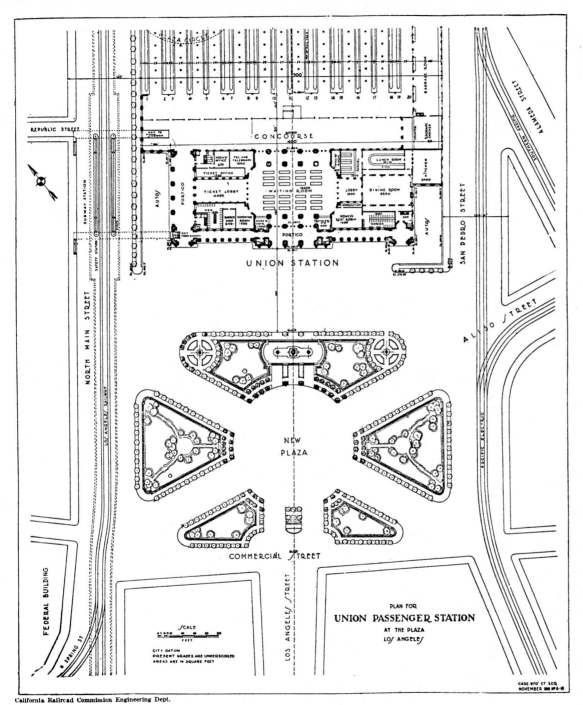

PLAN FOR
**UNION PASSENGER STATION**
AT THE PLAZA
LOS ANGELES

SCALE

FEET

CITY DATUM
PRESENT GRADES ARE UNDERSCORED
AREAS ARE IN SQUARE FEET

CASE 970' ET SEQ
NOVEMBER 1918 N°8-18

California Railroad Commission Engineering Dept.

IN ITS REPORT of 1919, the California Railroad Commission found this plan, from the firm of Leeds and Barnard, to be the most suitable. Main Street is shown widened to 120 feet, and a new plaza is created. Unfortunately, the plan also called for the complete obliteration of Olvera Street, today a cherished landmark.

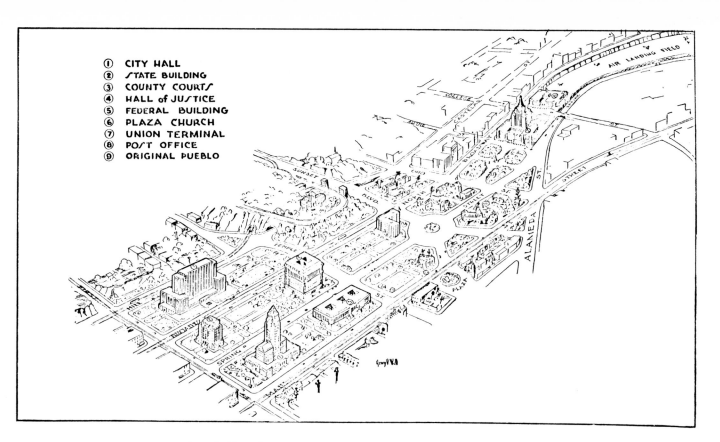

① CITY HALL
② STATE BUILDING
③ COUNTY COURTS
④ HALL of JUSTICE
⑤ FEDERAL BUILDING
⑥ PLAZA CHURCH
⑦ UNION TERMINAL
⑧ POST OFFICE
⑨ ORIGINAL PUEBLO

AS A WAY of keeping up with the times, one plan from the City Planning Department proposed putting an air strip on top of the tracks.
*From: Southwest Builder & Contractor*

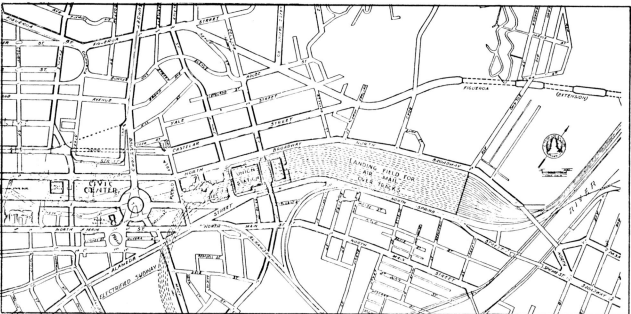

THE PLAZA                                      PROPOSED LOS ANGELES TERMINAL

THE EARLY PROPOSALS for a Terminal building were a far cry from what was eventually built. In 1919, when these were drawn, the California Railroad Commission felt that Union Station in Washington, D.C., represented the ideal in station design. *Sherman Foundation Library*

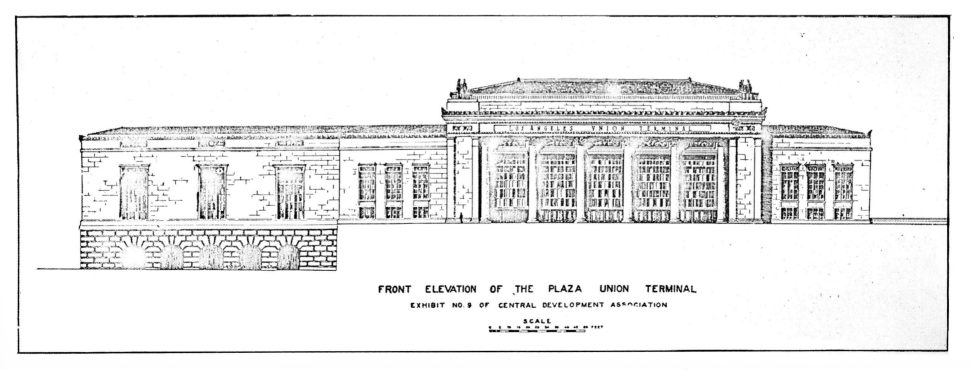

FRONT ELEVATION OF THE PLAZA UNION TERMINAL
EXHIBIT NO. 9 OF CENTRAL DEVELOPMENT ASSOCIATION

SCALE

The design finally selected for the terminal building was developed by a committee of architects from the three railroads, and by John and Donald Parkinson, who served as consulting architects. This drawing was prepared by the chief of terminal draftsmen, E.W. Markus, in early 1937, just before bids were taken for construction. *Ralph Melching*

# Men Behind the Station

THE CONSULTING ARCHITECTS, Donald B. Parkinson (left) and John Parkinson (right) were a distinguished team, whose previous credits included Saks Fifth Avenue in Beverly Hills and Bullocks Wilshire Department Store in Los Angeles.

FRANK SHAW, who was elected Mayor of Los Angeles in 1933, was responsible for allocating a million dollars in civic funds (raised from a gasoline tax) in the Union Station project, a move which broke the city's long stalemate with the railroads over the issue.

THE CRUSADING EFFORTS of Harry Chandler, publisher of the *Los Angeles Times*, helped to encourage public support for Union Station, especially when it seemed that most other publications were on the side of the railroads.

*All photos:*
*Security Pacific National Bank Historical collections*

COMPARE this photo with the one on page 57. The first phase of construction involved moving a massive 400,000 cubic yards of earth to raise tracks 12 feet above Macy Street (right) and 16 feet above Aliso Street (left). When this picture was taken in 1935, work had already begun on the 500-foot-long subway that would connect passengers with the tracks. Progress on the rest of the site was delayed as controversy raged over the location of the Post Office Terminal Annex.
*California Historical Society/Title Insurance (Los Angeles)*

# Construction Begins

THIS TUNNEL structure was built to carry the tracks across Macy St. into Union Station. During construction, the yellow streetcars on Los Angeles Railway's "B" line, like car #455 at right, ran on a "shoo-fly" detour. *Melching Brothers*

(Top right) A CONTRACTOR'S rail crane sets girders into supports for Union Pacific's access bridge across the Los Angeles River, toward Mission Tower (in the distance at left). (Middle) The new track pattern crossed over the site of the old Southern Pacific main line to Alameda Street. Continuity was assured by use of the new tracks at extreme right. The new trackage curves to the left to the terminal area. (Bottom) Looking toward the new trainsheds from the Vignes viaduct forms for the new Terminal Tower take shape. Much trackage was now laid out. *ALL: Melching Brothers*

The main building cost over 4½ million dollars to build, with Southern Pacific sharing 44% of the total, Santa Fe, 33% and Union Pacific, 23%.

THE PLATFORMS and "butterfly" canopies are fitted into place, as seen from the south (left) and the north (below, left). *Melching Brothers*

LOOKING toward the front of the station from the corner of Macy and Alameda streets, as work progresses (below and facing page). A steel skeleton supported walls of reinforced concrete. Below: *Melching Brothers* Facing page: *Southern Pacific*

THE WIRES were up, but the track had yet to be laid in the Pacific Electric coach yard, as crews finish laying concrete (above).
*Santa Fe Railway*

WITH THE DATE of completion always in doubt, somebody was prompted to write "We Hope" on the sign (above).
*Craig Rasmussen*

THE MAIN Waiting Room nears completion. *Santa Fe Railway*

# *Chapter 4*

# TRIUMPH IN STUCCO AND TILE

FROM THE OUTSIDE, the building's appearance suggests an early California mission. One notices the distinctive clock tower topped with a Moorish finial; the high arched windows and slanted red tile roofs; the arcades and patios that link it with low-rise buildings on either side and, finally, the setting—200 feet in from the street it faces—all of which seem at once to suggest something other than a railroad terminal.

By harking back to the region's Spanish heritage, architects H.L. Gilman, J.H. Christie and R.J. Wirth set out to give just such an impression. But in the station's interiors, their goal was modified to an extent by the desire to create an up-to-date facility and—partially—from their association with consulting architects John and Donald Parkinson. Consequently, many features are strongly redolent of 1930ish Art Deco—particularly the leather-upholstered settees, Venetian blinds, strip lighting and pencil Gothic signwork. As a result, Union Station is one of the few buildings ever built to successfully combine the two somewhat divergent styles into one, and, happily, its main building is as functional as it is unique.

*Faced with concrete, and separated from the street by a parking lot, the main building is a fine example of Mission Spanish and Mediterranean architecture.*

*This distinguished entryway is dominated by the bold, relief lettering on the marquee, and by the 50-foot-high arch. Rimmed with colored mosaics, this opening surrounds a smaller arch of ornamental concrete and patterned glass.*

*Union Pacific*

The main entrance

*William D. Middleton*

The station's entrance from the south arcade

The entrance vestibule, looking toward the
waiting room

The upper walls and ceilings of the station's larger rooms are faced with several varieties of acoustical tile. Something of a novelty when the station was built, these were effective in reducing "station echo"— a notorious feature of older terminals. Tile wainscoting, a thin strip of Belgium black marble and tavertine add color to the lower walls; red quarry tile covers most of the floors, except around the edges and along the center, where different strains of marble lie in a pattern suggesting a carpet runner. Outside light is filtered through the tall windows, which are fitted with amber cathedral glass and Venetian blinds. Night illumination comes from the impressive Spanish-type fixtures—10 feet in diameter—which hang suspended from the ceiling. Bronze-framed doors (like those below) lead to the patios.

*Mark Effle*

*William D. Middleton*

The main waiting room

The station's largest room is the one that outgoing passengers normally saw first—the ticket concourse. Here, the Spanish colonial decor is most fully expressed, as seen in the room's lofty height, the ornate wood-beamed ceiling, the chandeliers and tall, arched windows faced with iron grillwork. The 115-foot-long ticket counter—now only partially used by Amtrak—is fashioned from American black walnut, and contains small wickets at each seller's space.

*Mark Effle*

The ticket concourse leads straight ahead to rest rooms and an area just behind the far wall that was once a barber shop.

*Mark Effle*

The telephone room

In the days before direct dialing, all calls were handled through a switchboard housed behind the counter at left.

*Union Pacific*

The south patio

*The restaurant shows a Moorish influence, with a scale more intimate than the station's larger rooms. Cream-colored walls surround some mosaics, and the floor is composed of red, black and buff cement tile.*

*Mark Effle*

The former Fred Harvey restaurant

Although forlorn and empty today, this was once
the major dining facility in the station, seating 27
at the U-shaped counter (ahead) and 260 elsewhere.

*At this end of the station, the decor shifts markedly from Spanish Colonial to the functional, streamlined style more typical of 1930s modern. Especially noticeable is the fluorescent lighting. Still, even minor details, like the drinking fountains (lower left) warrant a showy display of colored mosaics.*

(Left) The train concourse, looking north toward the baggage rooms

(Below) The reception hall, looking south

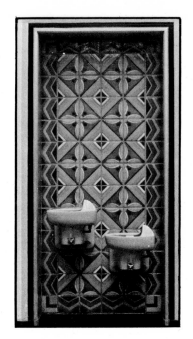

Ahead and to the left are rooms that once housed the Travelers' Aid offices.

***All photos: Mark Effle***

*Mark Effle*

The arrival and departure lobby

*Mark Effle*

The passenger subway leading to the train
platforms

*Chapter 5*

# UNDER AMTRAK

WHEN AMTRAK, the National Railroad Passenger Corporation, began operating on May 1, 1971, it was clear that the agency intended the frequency of service at Union Station to improve—and soon.

The first noticeable sign of change for the better was its positive attitude toward passenger trains, which were, after all, the only commodity Amtrak had to sell.

Getting people back to Union Station was Amtrak's biggest challenge, and soon media advertising began reminding Angelenos that yes, there was still a railroad station in Los Angeles providing comfortable, deluxe trains to many points.

Amtrak's "day one," however, marked the nadir of passenger train activity at Union Station. The major loss on that day was the Union Pacific's *City of Los Angeles,* which had become dubbed by rail insiders as the "City of Everything," because it had long since been combined with

AMTRAK'S OWN locomotives first pulled into Los Angeles in June 1973. Here are two of the 200-series units. *Mark Effle*

no less than three other Union Pacific streamliners—the Cities of *Portland, San Francisco* and *Denver*—on its journeys east.

That left only the Santa Fe's *Super Chief* to fly the Amtrak banner on the Chicago run. A secondary Santa Fe train on the same route, a remnant of the *Grand Canyon*, disappeared from the Union Station timetable on the same day, as did Southern Pacific's *San Joaquin Daylight,* by then a parody of its former grandeur.

The Southern Pacific, in fact, had cut back on passenger amenities several years before. It continued to provide safe and on-time basic transportation, but little else, while the Union Pacific and the Santa Fe kept up the old plush standards—at least on their premier trains. In 1970 and 1971, for instance, it was still not unknown for a gourmand to buy a ticket on the *Super* to San Bernardino, 60 miles out, just to enjoy a dinner on that famous train.

But now that Amtrak had taken over, what was it to do? As far as Union Station was concerned, there were no easy answers. First some cosmetic changes appeared. The depot staff was fitted in Amtrak's bright red blazers; red caps donned special Amtrak blue jumpsuits with a red and white stripe, and even the conductors and brakemen wore an Amtrak version of their traditional natty uniform. Then the cars were soon repainted from individual railroad liveries to Amtrak silver with its herald and blue and red stripes.

In terms of service, Southern Pacific's *Coast Daylight* was upgraded to a through San Diego-Seattle train which Amtrak, dipping into regional passenger train history, renamed the *Coast Starlight*. Although the through service to San Diego soon disappeared, the *Coast Starlight* continued to be a daily feature on Amtrak's West Coast system, where it remained extremely well patronized.

Amtrak kept Southern Pacific's *Sunset* to New Orleans, and even added some cast-off "hi-level" chair cars from

Santa Fe's *El Capitan.* The train enjoyed a healthy increase in patronage, but was still running only three times a week in 1979.

There were plans in 1978 to revive the famous *Lark* (though perhaps under a different name) between Los Angeles and the Bay Area, a move which would restore overnight service north out of the terminal. There was also talk of a revived *San Joaquin Daylight,* or at least a train using the same route over the Tehachapi Mountains to Bakersfield, and on to the Bay Area through the San Joaquin Valley.

Unquestionably, the biggest boost in the station's revival came as a result of stepped-up service to San Diego. As one of the most densely traveled urban corridors in the nation, it appeared that the Los Angeles-San Diego route might be an ideal proving ground for the kind of upgraded rail service that Amtrak had successfully developed between New York and Washington, D.C.

State Senator James S. Mills of San Diego saw it that way and, using every bit of political savvy he could muster, he persuaded Amtrak and Caltrans (as the California Department of Transportation has been known since the expansion of its responsibilities from strictly highways to all forms of transportation) to increase the frequency of its Los Angeles-San Diego service. Starting in 1974 with three trains per day each way, the service was increased first to four, then to five, and finally to six each way. And the public responded—with patronage tripling and still rising in 1979.

Suddenly in the late 1970s, there were a few times during most days when Union Station looked positively busy—shades of 1948! In fact, patronage between Los Angeles and San Diego was actually much heavier in 1979 than in 1948. Sadly, this was not the case on any other route, and outside

(Right) A MORNING *San Diegan* glides into its terminal track. All power for heating, cooling and appliances in the cars is generated in the locomotive, a departure from the steam boilers of yesteryear. ***Mark Effle***

of *San Diegan* train times, Union Station was also a very empty place in 1979. Furthermore, the post office had ceased using the loading facilities upstairs and R.E.A. Express (successor to the Railway Express Agency) had gone out of business.

Today, the station remains in remarkably good shape, a bit overdue for a paint job, perhaps, but nothing like the dungeons and crumbling ruins its older brothers in the east have become due to years of purposeful railroad neglect. It is, of course, largely through the emergence of Amtrak that the three railroad owners of Union Station have not tried to rid themselves of this financial drain. (At present, Amtrak leases much of the terminal, leaving only the handling of the switching towers, signals and track maintenance to the terminal corporation.)

There have been proposals to turn the station into a multi-model transportation center, or to move the passenger services closer to the tracks and adapt the front to either a shopping mall or a cultural center. In any case, one thing *is* certain: the building itself will at least be preserved, having been declared Los Angeles' 101st Historic Cultural Monument in 1972 by the Los Angeles Cultural Heritage Board. A similar designation from the federal government was pending at this writing.

Still, the fortunes of Los Angeles Union Passenger Terminal are, to a great extent, intertwined with the fate of Amtrak. If there is a renaissance of rail travel and the federal legislative branch retains a favorable political atmosphere, coming generations will continue to enjoy the beauties of this classic rail gateway to the City of the Angels.

(Above left) THESE TUBULAR-SHAPED "Amfleet" coaches stand ready for passengers on the San Diego route. Seating and interiors are a radical departure from traditional railroad design.

(Below left) Fortunately, scenes such as this are rare in today's station. ***BOTH: Mark Effle***

IN THE FORTY years since Union Station's opening, many Los Angeles landmarks have vanished, but the station itself has remained essentially unchanged. One modification was the Railway Express addition, built on the site of the former Pacific Electric service yard. *Jim Walker*

FORMS OF PUBLIC transportation serving Union Station's terminal loop changed dramatically in a quarter century. (Above) This mid-1950s view shows a No. 2 line trolley coach passing the loop as two streetcars await outbound passengers. In 1979 (right), Macy Street and the loop are devoid of tracks and trolley wires, and all service is provided by Southern California Rapid Transit District (RTD) diesel buses.
***BOTH: Mark Effle***

LOOKING BACK from the tracks, one landmark remains unchanged: the pointed City Hall building. (Left) The north patio and ticket concourse are at left, while the shorter, two-story wing at center houses Amtrak offices. (Below) The ends of the terminal tracks are just a few feet above the busy Santa Ana Freeway. The two-story structure at far center once contained the offices of Railway Express.
**BOTH: Mark Effle**

# APPENDIX

From 1939 to 1971, 89 station timetables were issued for use by employees. A new edition appeared each time one or more trains changed time, name, or was added or dropped. Ten of these have been reproduced on the following pages, and they give a clear indication of how the passenger train has fared in the last 40 years.

CONDENSED TIME TABLES CORRECTED TO MAY 7, 1939|

## SANTA FE R. R.
Uptown Office: 743 South Hill Street

| No. | East Leave L.A. | TRAIN | No. | West Arrive L.A. |
|---|---|---|---|---|
| 24 | 8:15 A.M. | **GRAND CANYON LTD.** (Kansas City and Chicago) | 23 | 8:15 P.M. |
| 20 | 11:30 A.M. | **THE CHIEF** (Kansas City and Chicago). Fastest daily train. | 19 | 11:50 A.M. |
| 22 | 1:30 P.M. | **EL CAPITAN** (Kansas City and Chicago.) DeLuxe Coaches and Diners—39¾ hours to Chicago. (Tues. and Fri. only)  (Mon. and Thurs. only) | 21 | 7:30 A.M. |
| 10 | 2:00 P.M. | **NAVAJO** (Kansas City and Chicago) | 9 | 12:05 P.M. |
| 4 | 7:15 P.M. | **CALIFORNIA LTD.** (Kansas City and Chicago) | 3 | 8:30 A.M. |
| 18 | 8:00 P.M. | **SUPER CHIEF** (Kansas City and Chicago, 39¾ hours) (Tues. and Fri. only)  (Mon. and Thurs. only) | 17 | 9:00 A.M. |
| 2 | 8:15 P.M. | **THE SCOUT** (Kansas City and Chicago) Three dining car meals, 90c per day. | 1 | 7:00 A.M. |
| 8 | 11:00 P.M. | **FAST MAIL & EXPRESS** (Kansas City and Chicago) | 7 | 8:00 P.M. |
| 72 | 9:15 A.M. | **SAN DIEGO** | 73 | 6:00 P.M. |
| 74 | 12:45 P.M. | **SAN DIEGAN** (DIESEL STREAMLINER) | 75 | 6:45 P.M. |
| 76 | 7:55 P.M. | **SAN DIEGO** (DIESEL STREAMLINER) | 77 | 10:30 P.M. |
| 78 | 11:30 P.M. | **SAN DIEGAN** | 71 | 10:30 A.M. |
| 42 | 9:40 A.M. | Via Pasa.-San Bdno.          Via Riverside and Fullerton | 51 | 9:10 A.M. |
| 54 | 5:20 P.M. | Via Fullerton-San Bdno.      Via Riverside and Fullerton | 53 | 3:55 P.M. |

## SOUTHERN PACIFIC R. R.
Uptown Office: 212 West Seventh Street

| No. | East | TRAIN | No. | West |
|---|---|---|---|---|
| 2 | 9:45 A.M. | **SUNSET LTD.** (Phoenix-San Antonio-Houston-New Orleans) | 1 | 4:30 P.M. |
| 6 | 8:15 P.M. | **ARGONAUT** (El Paso-San Antonio-Houston-New Orleans) | 5 | 7:30 A.M. |
| 44 | 8:00 P.M. | **CALIFORNIAN** (El Paso-K.C.-Chicago) | 43 | 7:10 A.M. |
| 4 | 8:10 P.M. | **GOLDEN STATE LTD.** (Yuma-Phoenix-El Paso-K.C.-Mpls.-Chi. | 3 | 8:30 A.M. |
| 368 | 9:30 P.M. | **IMPERIAL VALLEY LOCAL** (Calexico) | 367 | 5:15 A.M. |
| | North | | | South |
| 51 | 7:45 A.M. | **SAN JOAQUIN FLYER** (San Francisco)  (Valley) | 52 | 10:05 P.M. |
| 99 | 8:15 A.M. | **DAYLIGHT LTD.** (San Francisco, Streamline)  (Coast) | 98 | 6:00 P.M. |
| 71 | 8:20 A.M. | **COAST PASSENGER**  (Coast) | 72 | 10:00 P.M. |
| 25 | 6:00 P.M. | **OWL** (Oakland—via Bakersfield)  (Valley) | 26 | 8:35 A.M. |
| 69 | 7:00 P.M. | **COASTER** (San Francisco)  (Coast) | 70 | 8:00 A.M. |
| 59 | 7:45 P.M. | **WEST COAST** (Fresno-Sacramento-Portland)  (Valley) | 60 | 8:50 A.M. |
| 1 | 8:00 P.M. | **SUNSET LTD.** (San Francisco)  (Coast) | 2 | 8:10 A.M. |
| 55 | 8:25 P.M. | **TEHACHAPI** (Fresno-Oakland)  (Valley) | 56 | 6:40 A.M. |
| 75 | 9:00 P.M. | **LARK** (San Francisco)  (Coast) | 76 | 9:00 A.M. |

## UNION PACIFIC R. R.
Uptown Office: Sixth and Olive Streets

| No. | East | TRAIN | No. | West |
|---|---|---|---|---|
| 14 | 8:00 A.M. | **PACIFIC LIMITED** (Butte, Denver, Kansas City, St. Louis, Omaha, Mpls.-St. Paul, Chicago.) | 21 | 8:45 P.M. |
| 104* | 6:30 P.M. | **CITY OF LOS ANGELES,** Streamliner, 39¾ hours to Chi. *17 Car Train departs 3rd, 9th, 15th, 21st, 27. *12 Car Train departs 6th, 12th, 18th, 24th, and last day of each month. †17 Car Train arrives 2nd, 8th, 14th, 20th, 26th. †12 Car Train arrives 5th, 11th, 17th, 23rd, 29th day of each month. | 103† | 8:00 A.M. |
| 8 | 8:00 P.M. | **LOS ANGELES LIMITED,** Exclusive, All Standard Pullman Train. Boulder Dam, Zion Nat. Park, Sun Valley, Butte, Denver, K.C., Omaha, St. Louis, Mpls.-St. Paul, Chicago. | 7 | 8:30 A.M. |
| 818 | 8:05 P.M. | **THE CHALLENGER,** "Everybody's Limited" Tourist Pullman, Coaches, Economy Meals. (Boulder Dam, Zion Nat. Park, Sun Valley, Butte, Denver, K.C., Omaha, St. Louis, Mpls.-St. Paul, Chicago.) | 717 | 8:35 A.M. |
| 6 | 10:30 P.M. | **CALIFORNIA FAST MAIL,** Coach passengers. (Only to operating stops.) | 5 | 5:50 P.M. |

## LOS ANGELES UNION PASSENGER TERMINAL
# TIME TABLE
### Effective Jan. 25, 1942

| ARRIVING | | | LEAVING | | |
|---|---|---|---|---|---|
| **TRAIN** | **TIME** | **NAME** | **TRAIN** | **TIME** | **NAME** |
| SP 56 | 4:00 AM | *Tehachapi* | SP 71 | 7:10 AM | *S. F. Passenger* |
| SP 43 | 7:05 AM | *Californian* | AT 70 | 8:00 AM | *San Diegan* |
| SP 5 | 7:30 AM | *Argonaut* | AT 24 | 8:15 AM | *Grand Canyon Ltd.* |
| AT 21 | ▲7:30 AM | *El Capitan* | SP 99 | 8:15 AM | *Morning Daylight* |
| UP 37 | 7:40 AM | *Los Angeles Ltd.* | SP 51 | 9:00 AM | *San Joaquin Daylight* |
| UP 7 | 7:50 AM | *Challenger* | AT 72 | 9:20 AM | *San Diego Local* |
| SP 70 | 7:50 AM | *Coaster* | SP 2 | 9:45 AM | *Sunset Limited* |
| UP 103 | *8:00 AM | *City of Los Angeles* | AT 42 | 9:50 AM | *Motor* |
| AT 1 | 8:30 AM | *Scout* | UP 24 | 11:00 AM | *Pacific Limited* |
| SP 26 | 8:35 AM | *Owl* | AT 20 | 11:30 AM | *Chief* |
| SP 60 | 8:45 AM | *West Coast* | AT 74 | 12:30 PM | *San Diegan* |
| SP 76 | 9:00 AM | *Lark* | AT 22 | •1:30 PM | *El Capitan* |
| AT 17 | ▲9:00 AM | *Super Chief* | AT 76 | 5:00 PM | *San Diegan* |
| AT 51 | 9:10 AM | *Motor* | AT 54 | 5:20 PM | *Motor* |
| AT 71 | 10:30 AM | *San Diegan* | SP 25 | 6:00 PM | *Owl* |
| AT 3 | 11:40 AM | *California Limited* | UP 104 | †6:30 PM | *City of Los Angeles* |
| AT 19 | 11:50 AM | *Chief* | SP 69 | 7:00 PM | *Coaster* |
| AT 73 | 3:15 PM | *San Diegan* | AT 4 | 7:15 PM | *California Limited* |
| AT 53 | 4:00 PM | *Motor* | SP 59 | 7:45 PM | *West Coast* |
| SP 1 | 4:30 PM | *Sunset Limited* | AT 18 | •8:00 PM | *Super Chief* |
| SP 98 | 5:45 PM | *Morning Daylight* | SP 44 | 8:00 PM | *Californian* |
| AT 75 | 6:45 PM | *San Diegan* | UP 38 | 8:00 PM | *Los Angeles Ltd.* |
| SP 3 | 7:25 PM | *Golden State Ltd.* | UP 8 | 8:05 PM | *Challenger* |
| SP 52 | 7:40 PM | *San Joaquin Daylight* | SP 4 | 8:10 PM | *Golden State Ltd.* |
| AT 23 | 7:40 PM | *Grand Canyon Ltd.* | SP 6 | 8:15 PM | *Argonaut* |
| AT 7 | 8:00 PM | *Fast Mail & Exp.* | AT 2 | 8:15 PM | *Scout* |
| UP 23 | 10:30 PM | *Pacific Limited* | SP 55 | 8:25 PM | *Tehachapi* |
| AT 77 | 10:30 PM | *San Diego Local* | SP 75 | 9:00 PM | *Lark* |
| SP 72 | 10:35 PM | *L. A. Passenger* | AT 78 | 9:00 PM | *San Diegan* |
| AT 79 | 11:15 PM | *San Diegan* | AT 8 | 11:00 PM | *Fast Mail & Exp* |

▲ Monday and Thursday only.

• 2nd, 5th, 8th, 11th, 14th, 17th, 20th, 23rd, 26th, 29th of each month.

• Tuesday and Friday only.

† 3rd, 6th, 9th, 12th, 15th, 18th, 21st, 24th 27th and last day of each month.


## LOS ANGELES UNION PASSENGER TERMINAL
# TIME TABLE
### Effective June 2, 1946

| ARRIVING | | | LEAVING | | |
|---|---|---|---|---|---|
| **TRAIN** | **TIME** | **NAME** | **TRAIN** | **TIME** | **NAME** |
| SP 72 | 12:01 AM | *L. A. Passenger* | AT 70 | 12:30 AM | *San Diego Local* |
| SP 47 | 1:45 AM | *Chicago Passenger* | SP 71 | 6:00 AM | *S. F. Passenger* |
| SP 56 | 6:00 AM | *Tehachapi* | AT 72 | 7:45 AM | *San Diegan* |
| UP 37 | 7:00 AM | *Pony Express* | UP 44 | 8:00 AM | *Passenger* |
| SP 5 | 7:00 AM | *Argonaut* | SP 99 | 8:15 AM | *Morning Daylight* |
| SP 43 | 7.10 AM | *Californian* | SP 51 | 8:25 AM | *San Joaquin Daylight* |
| UP 7 | 7:10 AM | *Challenger* | AT 24 | 9:00 AM | *Grand Canyon Ltd.* |
| AT 1 | 7:15 AM | *Scout* | AT 42 | 9:50 AM | *Motor* |
| AT 21 | ▼7:30 AM | *El Capitan* | UP 4 | 10:00 AM | *Transcontinental* |
| SP 70 | 8:00 AM | *Coaster* | SP 4 | 11:15 AM | *Golden State Limited* |
| AT 3 | 8:00 AM | *California Limited* | AT 74 | 11:30 AM | *San Diegan* |
| SP 58 | 8:35 AM | *Owl* | UP 2 | 11:30 AM | *Los Angeles Limited* |
| AT 17 | ▼8:45 AM | *Super Chief* | AT 20 | 12:01 PM | *Chief* |
| SP 60 | 8:45 AM | *West Coast* | SP 97 | 12:15 PM | *Noon Daylight* |
| SP 76 | 9:00 AM | *Lark* | SP 2 | 12:30 PM | *Sunset Limited* |
| AT 51 | 9:10 AM | *Motor* | AT 22 | •1:30 PM | *El Capitan* |
| UP 103 | *9:15 AM | *City of Los Angeles* | AT 124 | 2:30 PM | *El Tovar* |
| SP 1 | 9:25 AM | *Sunset Limited* | AT 76 | 3:15 PM | *San Diegan* |
| AT 19 | 10:00 AM | *Chief* | UP 104 | †4:30 PM | *City of Los Angeles* |
| UP 3 | 10:20 AM | *Transcontinental* | SP 57 | 5:50 PM | *Owl* |
| AT 71 | 10:30 AM | *San Diegan* | AT 54 | 6:25 PM | *Motor* |
| AT 123 | 11:00 AM | *El. Tovar* | AT 4 | 7:00 PM | *California Limited* |
| AT 73 | 2:15 PM | *San Diegan* | SP 59 | 7:30 PM | *West Coast* |
| UP 1 | 2:20 PM | *Los Angeles Limited* | SP 69 | 7:55 PM | *Coaster* |
| AT 75 | 4:00 PM | *San Diego Local* | AT 18 | •8:00 PM | *Super Chief* |
| AT 53 | 5:55 PM | *Motor* | AT 78 | 8:00 PM | *San Diegan* |
| SP 98 | 6:00 PM | *Morning Daylight* | SP 44 | 8:00 PM | *Californian* |
| AT 23 | 6:00 PM | *Grand Canyon Ltd.* | AT 2 | 8:15 PM | *Scout* |
| AT 77 | 6:45 PM | *San Diegan* | SP 6 | 8:20 PM | *Argonaut* |
| UP 43 | 7:45 PM | *Passenger* | SP 55 | 8:30 PM | *Tehachapi* |
| SP 52 | 7:50 PM | *San Joaquin Daylight* | UP 38 | 8:30 PM | *Pony Express* |
| AT 7 | 8:00 PM | *Mail and Express* | UP 8 | 8:35 PM | *Challenger* |
| SP 3 | 8:45 PM | *Golden State Limited* | SP 75 | 9:00 PM | *Lark* |
| AT 79 | 9:45 PM | *San Diegan* | SP 48 | 9:10 PM | *Chicago Passenger* |
| SP 96 | 9:55 PM | *Noon Daylight* | AT 8 | 11:30 PM | *Mail and Express* |

▼ Monday and Thursday only.

* 2nd, 5th, 8th, 11th, 14th, 17th, 20th, 23rd, 26th, 29th of each month.

• Tuesday and Friday only.

† 3rd, 6th, 9th, 12th, 15th, 18th, 21st, 24th, 27th and last day of each month.

# LOS ANGELES UNION PASSENGER TERMINAL

## TIME TABLE

### Effective September 24, 1950

| **Pacific Standard Time** ARRIVING | | | **Pacific Standard Time** LEAVING | | |
|---|---|---|---|---|---|
| TRAIN | TIME | NAME | TRAIN | TIME | NAME |
| SP 56 | 6:00 AM | *Tehachapi* | AT 70 | 12:30 AM | *San Diego Local* |
| SP 94 | 6:45 AM | *Starlight* | SP 71 | 1:00 AM | *S. F. Passenger* |
| UP 37 | 7:00 AM | *Pony Express* | SP 40 | 7:30 AM | *Imperial* |
| AT 3 | 7:00 AM | *California Limited* | SP 51 | 7:50 AM | *San Joaquin Daylight* |
| SP 43 | 7:05 AM | *Cherokee* | AT 72 | 8:00 AM | *San Diegan* |
| AT 21 | 7:30 AM | *El Capitan* | SP 99 | 8:15 AM | *Morning Daylight* |
| SP 3 | 7:35 AM | *Golden State* | AT 42 | 10:10 AM | *Local* |
| AT 45 | 8:15 AM | *Local* | UP 4 | 11:00 AM | *Utahn* |
| AT 19 | 8:30 AM | *Chief* | AT 74 | 11:30 AM | *San Diegan* |
| AT 17 | 8:45 AM | *Super Chief* | UP 2 | 12:01 PM | *Los Angeles Limited* |
| SP 60 | 8:50 AM | *West Coast* | AT 20 | 12:30 PM | *Chief* |
| SP 76 | 9:00 AM | *Lark* | SP 4 | 1:30 PM | *Golden State* |
| UP 103 | 9:00 AM | *City of Los Angeles* | AT 22 | 1:30 PM | *El Capitan* |
| AT 51 | 9:30 AM | *Local* | AT 124 | 1:30 PM | *Grand Canyon* |
| AT 123 | 10:25 AM | *Grand Canyon* | AT 24 | 1:40 PM | *Grand Canyon* |
| AT 71 | 10:30 AM | *San Diegan* | AT 76 | 3:30 PM | *San Diegan* |
| AT 23 | 10:40 AM | *Grand Canyon* | UP 104 | 5:00 PM | *City of Los Angeles* |
| UP 1 | 10:40 AM | *Los Angeles Limited* | AT 54 | 5:30 PM | *Local* |
| SP 58 | 10:45 AM | *Owl* | SP 57 | 5:40 PM | *Owl* |
| AT 73 | 2:30 PM | *San Diegan* | AT 4 | 6:15 PM | *California Limited* |
| SP 5 | 3:45 PM | *Argonaut* | AT 78 | 7:30 PM | *San Diegan* |
| UP 3 | 4:00 PM | *Utahn* | SP 59 | 7:30 PM | *West Coast* |
| SP 72 | 4:15 PM | *L. A. Passenger* | UP 38 | 7:30 PM | *Pony Express* |
| SP 1 | 4:30 PM | *Sunset* | AT 18 | 8:00 PM | *Super Chief* |
| AT 75 | 5:45 PM | *San Diego Local* | SP 95 | 8:00 PM | *Starlight* |
| AT 77 | 6:00 PM | *San Diegan* | SP 2 | 8:00 PM | *Sunset* |
| SP 98 | 6:00 PM | *Morning Daylight* | SP 44 | 8:05 PM | *Cherokee* |
| AT 7 | 7:00 PM | *Mail and Express* | SP 6 | 8:30 PM | *Argonaut* |
| SP 52 | 7:20 PM | *San Joaquin Daylight* | SP 75 | 9:00 PM | *Lark* |
| AT 79 | 10:00 PM | *San Diegan* | SP 55 | 9:40 PM | *Tehachapi* |
| SP 39 | 10:55 PM | *Imperial* | AT 8 | 11:30 PM | *Mail and Express* |

# LOS ANGELES UNION PASSENGER TERMINAL

## TIME TABLE

### Effective April 24, 1955

| **Pacific Standard Time** ARRIVING | | | **Pacific Standard Time** LEAVING | | |
|---|---|---|---|---|---|
| TRAIN | TIME | NAME | TRAIN | TIME | NAME |
| UP 5 | 5:30 AM | *Mail and Express* | SP 91 | 12:01 AM | *S. F. Passenger* |
| SP 94 | 5:45 AM | *Starlight* | SP 51 | 6:55 AM | *San Joaquin Daylight* |
| SP 39 | 6:30 AM | *Imperial* | SP 99 | 7:15 AM | *Coast Daylight* |
| SP 3 | 7:00 AM | *Golden State* | AT 72 | 7:45 AM | *San Diegan* |
| AT 21 | 7:15 AM | *El Capitan* | AT 80 | 9:00 AM | *San Diego Passenger* |
| SP 60 | 7:15 AM | *West Coast* | UP 10 | 10:30 AM | *City of St. Louis* |
| SP 76 | 8:00 AM | *Lark* | AT 74 | 11:30 AM | *San Diegan* |
| AT 17 | 8:30 AM | *Super Chief* | AT 124 | 12:30 PM | *Grand Canyon* |
| AT 81 | 8:30 AM | *San Diego Passenger* | AT 22 | 1:30 PM | *El Capitan* |
| UP 103 | 9:30 AM | *City of Los Angeles* | SP 4 | 1:30 PM | *Golden State* |
| AT 71 | 10:30 AM | *San Diegan* | UP 108 | 2:00 PM | *Challenger* |
| SP 58 | 10:30 AM | *Owl* | AT 20 | 3:00 PM | *Chief* |
| AT 123 | 10:45 AM | *Grand Canyon* | AT 76 | 3:15 PM | *San Diegan* |
| AT 73 | 2:15 PM | *San Diegan* | AT 82 | 4:15 PM | *San Diego Passenger* |
| UP 9 | 3:15 PM | *City of St. Louis* | UP 104 | 4:30 PM | *City of Los Angeles* |
| SP 5 | 3:15 PM | *Argonaut* | SP 57 | 6:00 PM | *Owl* |
| SP 83 | 3:30 PM | *San Diego Passenger* | SP 95 | 6:45 PM | *Starlight* |
| SP 1 | 4:15 PM | *Sunset* | SP 59 | 6:55 PM | *West Coast* |
| AT 75 | 4:30 PM | *San Diego Local* | AT 18 | 7:00 PM | *Super Chief* |
| SP 90 | 4:30 PM | *L. A. Passenger* | AT 78 | 8:00 PM | *San Diegan* |
| SP 98 | 5:00 PM | *Coast Daylight* | SP 2 | 8:00 PM | *Sunset* |
| AT 77 | 5:30 PM | *San Diegan* | SP 75 | 8:00 PM | *Lark* |
| AT 7 | 6:30 PM | *Mail & Express* | SP 40 | 8:10 PM | *Imperial* |
| SP 52 | 7:05 PM | *San Joaquin Daylight* | SP 6 | 9:00 PM | *Argonaut* |
| AT 3 | 7:30 PM | *Passenger* | UP 6 | 10:00 PM | *Mail & Express* |
| AT 79 | 9:30 PM | *San Diegan* | AT 70 | 11:15 PM | *San Diego Local* |
| AT 19 | 10:30 PM | *Chief* | AT 4 | 11:30 PM | *Passenger* |
| UP 107 | 10:30 PM | *Challenger* | AT 8 | 11:45 PM | *Mail & Express* |

# LOS ANGELES UNION PASSENGER TERMINAL
## TIME TABLE
### Effective September 24, 1961

| **Pacific Standard Time ARRIVING** | | | **Pacific Standard Time LEAVING** | | |
|---|---|---|---|---|---|
| **TRAIN** | **TIME** | **NAME** | **TRAIN** | **TIME** | **NAME** |
| UP 5 | 5:00 AM | Passenger | AT 8 | 12:30 AM | Mail and Express |
| AT 17 | 8:00 AM | Super Chief– El Capitan | SP 40 | 1:00 AM | Passenger |
| SP 76 | 8:30 AM | Lark | AT 70 | 1:45 AM | San Diegan |
| SP 3 | 8:30 AM | Golden State | SP 51 | 6:30 AM | San Joaquin Daylight |
| *AT 71 | 8:45 AM | San Diegan | AT 72 | 7:05 AM | San Diegan |
| UP 103 | 10:15 AM | Domeliner City of Los Angeles | SP 99 | 8:15 AM | Coast Daylight |
| | | | %UP 116 | 9:00 AM | City of Las Vegas |
| | | | AT 74 | 10:20 AM | San Diegan |
| SP 58 | 10:20 AM | Owl | AT 20 | 12:01 PM | Chief |
| AT 73 | 10:45 AM | San Diegan | AT 124 | 1:15 PM | Grand Canyon |
| AT 123 | 12:10 PM | Grand Canyon | SP 4 | 1:30 PM | Golden State |
| UP 9 | 1:00 PM | City of St. Louis | UP 10 | 1:45 PM | City of St. Louis |
| SP 90 | 3:10 PM | L. A. Passenger | AT 76 | 2:30 PM | San Diegan |
| AT 75 | 3:45 PM | San Diegan | UP 104 | 3:45 PM | Domeliner City of Los Angeles |
| SP 1 | 5:15 PM | Sunset | | | |
| SP 98 | 6:05 PM | Coast Daylight | AT 78 | 5:45 PM | San Diegan |
| SP 52 | 7:00 PM | San Joaquin Daylight | SP 57 | 6:20 PM | Owl |
| AT 77 | 7:25 PM | San Diegan | AT 18 | 8:00 PM | Super Chief– El Capitan |
| AT 7 | 7:30 PM | Mail and Express | | | |
| #AT 79 | 9:55 PM | San Diegan | SP 2 | 8:00 PM | Sunset |
| SP 39 | 11:00 PM | Passenger | #AT 80 | 8:30 PM | San Diegan |
| AT 19 | 11:15 PM | Chief | SP 75 | 9:00 PM | Lark |
| AT 81 | 11:50 PM | San Diegan | UP 6 | 10:15 PM | Passenger |
| @UP 115 | 11:59 PM | City of Las Vegas | SP 91 | 11:30 PM | S. F. Passenger |

| **BUS** | **TIME** | | **BUS** | **TIME** | |
|---|---|---|---|---|---|
| SFT | 3:25 AM | From Bakersfield | SFT | 8:15 AM | Via Hollywood for Bakersfield |
| SFT | 5:20 PM | From Bakersfield | SFT | 10:30 AM | Via Pasadena for Bakersfield |
| | | | SFT | 11:00 AM | Via Hollywood for Bakersfield |

* Daily except Sundays and Holidays.
\# Sundays and Holidays only.
@ Effective September 30, Fridays and Sundays only.
% Effective September 30, Fridays and Saturdays only.

*IT TAKES LONGER TO REPORT AN ACCIDENT THAN TO PREVENT ONE.*

---

# LOS ANGELES UNION PASSENGER TERMINAL
## TIME TABLE
### Effective April 25, 1965

| **Pacific Standard Time ARRIVING** | | | **Pacific Standard Time LEAVING** | | |
|---|---|---|---|---|---|
| **TRAIN** | **TIME** | **NAME** | **TRAIN** | **TIME** | **NAME** |
| SP 39 | 3:00 AM | Mail | AT 8 | 12:30 AM | Mail and Express |
| UP 5 | 5:00 AM | Passenger | AT 72 | 6:00 AM | San Diegan |
| SP 76 | 7:30 AM | Lark | SP 51 | 6:25 AM | San Joaquin Daylight |
| *AT 71 | 7:45 AM | San Diegan | @UP 116 | 8:00 AM | Las Vegas Holiday Special |
| AT 17 | 8:00 AM | Super Chief– El Capitan | SP 99 | 9:15 AM | Coast Daylight |
| SP 3 | 8:15 AM | Sunset– Golden State | AT 74 | 9:15 AM | San Diegan |
| | | | AT 20 | 11:30 AM | Chief |
| AT 73 | 9:55 AM | San Diegan | AT 76 | 1:15 PM | San Diegan |
| AT 23 | 12:10 PM | Grand Canyon | UP 104 | 1:30 PM | City of Los Angeles– City of St. Louis |
| UP 103 | 12:30 PM | City of Los Angeles– City of St. Louis | AT 24 | 1:45 PM | Grand Canyon |
| SP 154 | 2:10 PM | Mail | AT 78 | 4:45 PM | San Diegan |
| AT 75 | 2:55 PM | San Diegan | AT 18 | 8:00 PM | Super Chief– El Capitan |
| SP 98 | 6:15 PM | Coast Daylight | | | |
| SP 52 | 6:35 PM | San Joaquin Daylight | SP 75 | 8:00 PM | Lark |
| AT 77 | 7:10 PM | San Diegan | #AT 80 | 8:15 PM | San Diegan |
| AT 7 | 7:30 PM | Mail and Express | SP 2 | 8:30 PM | Sunset– Golden State |
| #AT 79 | 8:40 PM | San Diegan | | | |
| @UP 115 | 10:15 PM | Las Vegas Holiday Special | SP 151 | 10:00 PM | Mail |
| | | | UP 6 | 10:15 PM | Passenger |
| AT 19 | 11:15 PM | Chief | SP 40 | 11:30 PM | Mail |

| **BUS** | **TIME** | | **BUS** | **TIME** | |
|---|---|---|---|---|---|
| SFT | 1:30 AM | From Bakersfield | SFT | 8:15 AM | Via Pasadena for Bakersfield |
| SFT | 4:10 PM | From Bakersfield | SFT | 8:30 AM | Via Hollywood for Bakersfield |
| SFT | 4:30 PM | From Bakersfield | SFT | 5:00 PM | Via Hollywood for Bakersfield |

* Daily except Sundays and Holidays.
\# Sundays and Holidays only.
@ Fridays and Sundays only.

*THERE IS A SAFE WAY; DO IT THAT WAY.*

# LOS ANGELES UNION PASSENGER TERMINAL

# TIME TABLE

Effective March 23, 1969

| Pacific Standard Time ARRIVING | | | | Pacific Standard Time LEAVING | | |
|---|---|---|---|---|---|---|
| TRAIN | TIME | NAME | | TRAIN | TIME | NAME |
| AT 23 | 6:00 AM | | | SP 51 | 7:00 AM | *San Joaquin Daylight* |
| SP 1 | 6:30 AM | *Sunset* | | AT 74 | 7:30 AM | *San Diegan* |
| AT 17 | 9:00 AM | *Super Chief- El Capitan* | | SP 99 | 8:30 AM | *Coast Daylight* |
| AT 73 | 9:55 AM | *San Diegan* | | AT 76 | 11:00 AM | *San Diegan* |
| UP 103 | 12:30 PM | *City of Los Angeles- City of Kansas City* | | UP 104 | 2:30 PM | *City of Los Angeles- City of Kansas City* |
| AT 75 | 2:25 PM | *San Diegan* | | AT 18 | 7:30 PM | *Super Chief- El Capitan* |
| AT 77 | 6:55 PM | *San Diegan* | | AT 78 | 7:45 PM | *San Diegan* |
| SP 52 | 7:50 PM | *San Joaquin Daylight* | | AT 24 | 9:00 PM | |
| SP 98 | 8:05 PM | *Coast Daylight* | | ~~UP 6~~ | ~~9:00 PM~~ | ~~*Passenger*~~ |
| ~~UP 5~~ | ~~11:45 PM~~ | ~~*Passenger*~~ | | SP 2 | 10:00 PM | *Sunset* |

*SAFE WAYS ARE HAPPY WAYS.*

LOS ANGELES UNION PASSENGER TERMINAL

NATIONAL RAILROAD PASSENGER CORPORATION

TIME TABLE NO. 90

Effective May 1, 1971

| Pacific Standard Time ARRIVING | | | | Pacific Standard Time LEAVING | | |
|---|---|---|---|---|---|---|
| NRPC TRAIN | TIME | NAME | NRPC TRAIN | TIME | NAME |
| SP 1 (Sun-Wed-Fri) | 7:30 AM | Sunset | AT 76 | 10:00 AM | San Diegan |
| | | | SP 99 | 10:15 AM | Coast Daylight |
| AT 17 | 9:00 AM | Super Chief El Capit. | | (Mon-Tues-Thur-Sat) | |
| | | | SP 99-12 | 10:15 AM | San Diego-Seattle |
| AT 12-79 (Sun-Wed-Fri) | 9:45 AM | San Diego- | | (Sun-Wed-Fri) | |
| | | | AT 78 | 6:00 PM | San Diegan |
| AT 75 | 11:55 AM | San Diegan | AT 18 | 7:30 PM | Super Chief - El Capitan |
| AT 77 | 6:55 PM | San Diegan | | | |
| SP 98 (Mon-Wed-Thur-Sat) | 7:15 PM | Coast Dayl | AT 80-11 | 7:45 PM | Seattle-San Diego |
| | | | | (Sun-Tues-Fri) | |
| SP 11-98 (Sun-Tues-Fri) | 7:15 PM | Seattle-Sa | SP 2 | 10:00 PM | Sunset |
| | | | | (Sun-Tues-Fri) | |

AMTRAK

FOR INFORMATION OF EMPLOYES ONLY.

L. W. GARRISON
Superintendent

*Except for the discontinuance of Union Pacific trains 5 and 6 in 1969, these trains ran until Amtrak assumed operation.*

# LOS ANGELES UNION PASSENGER TERMINAL

# TIME TABLE

### as of January 1979

| Pacific Standard Time | | | | Pacific Standard Time | | |
| ARRIVING | | | | LEAVING | | |
| TRAIN | TIME | NAME | | TRAIN | TIME | NAME |
| --- | --- | --- | --- | --- | --- | --- |
| 1 | 7:40 AM | *Sunset (W, F, Su)* | | 770 | 8:30 AM | *San Diegan* |
| 781 | 7:50 AM | *San Diegan (exc Sun)* | | 14 | 10:00 AM | *The Coast Starlight* |
| 3 | 9:05 AM | *Southwest Limited* | | 772 | 10:30 AM | *San Diegan* |
| 771 | 9:35 AM | *San Diegan* | | 774 | 1:30 PM | *San Diegan* |
| 773 | 12:10 PM | *San Diegan* | | 776 | 4:30 PM | *San Diegan (exc Sat)* |
| 775 | 3:35 PM | *San Diegan* | | 780 | 5:30 PM | *San Diegan* |
| 11 | 6:55 PM | *The Coast Starlight* | | 4 | 7:30 PM | *Southwest Limited* |
| 777 | 7:05 PM | *San Diegan* | | 778 | 8:30 PM | *San Diegan* |
| 779 | 10:05 PM | *San Diegan* | | 2 | 10:30 PM | *Sunset (Su, Tu, F)* |

# ACKNOWLEDGEMENTS

*We wish to thank the following individuals and organizations who allowed us to use their photographs, and who gave us much-needed assistance in gathering information about the station:*

Gerald M. Best
California Historical Society (Los Angeles)
David Cameron
Donald Duke
Mark Effle
Bill Kennedy
Stan Kistler
Ralph and Wayne Melching
William D. Middleton
Craig Rasmussen
Santa Fe Railway—Gene Flohrschutz
Security-Pacific National Bank—Victor Plukas
Sherman Foundation Library—Dr. William Hendricks
Southern Pacific—Richard Hall
Union Pacific—Al Krieg
Union Station—Bob Pfister
Ed Von Nordeck